SECRETS OF INTERNATIONAL IDENTITY CHANGE

*

For A Free Copy Of Our Complete Book Catalog, Write:
EDEN PRESS
P.O. Box 8410 Fountain Valley, CA 92728

Secrets of
INTERNATIONAL IDENTITY CHANGE

New I.D. in Canada, England, Australia, and New Zealand

Tony Newborn

PALADIN PRESS
BOULDER, COLORADO

Secrets of International Identity Change
New I.D. in Canada, England, Australia, and New Zealand
by Tony Newborn

Copyright © 1989 by Tony Newborn

ISBN 0-87364-532-4
Printed in the United States of America

Published by Paladin Press, a division of
Paladin Enterprises, Inc., P.O. Box 1307,
Boulder, Colorado 80306, USA.
(303) 443-7250

Direct inquiries and/or orders to the above address.

All rights reserved. Except for use in a review, no
portion of this book may be reproduced in any form
without the express written permission of the publisher.

Neither the author nor the publisher assumes
any responsibility for the use or misuse of
information contained in this book.

CONTENTS

Introduction...1

1
England...3

2
Australia...35

3
New Zealand...57

4
Canada...81

5
General Techniques and Information...85

INTRODUCTION

So, you've made a few mistakes, had more than your share of bad luck, and your debts outweigh your income. Taxes, alimony, credit repayments; everything is closing in, and unless you can get something new together fast, you'll go under—for good! What if the government decides to up your income tax, reduce the number of firearms that any one person can own, or just generally tightens the noose around certain freedom-loving necks? They know who you are, how you voted, and where you can be found in the event your opinons or actions "threaten" the stability of the system. So what can you do? How can you break away from such unwanted attention and start again? And how can you ensure that this new-found freedom will not again be violated?

The answers are here.

Paper Tripping Overseas enables you to start again with a clean slate. Written especially for use outside the United States, it shows how you can obtain all the legal and valid documents you might need to support an I.D. change. Birth certificate, driver's license, and credit cards are all yours for the asking. And so are a British passport and medical card—two of the most important documents in the world today.

Paper Tripping Overseas explains how you can obtain such documents, prove to everyone's satisfaction that you are who you say you are, and, most importantly, make sure that your past never catches up with you.

Different countries have different rules and regulations pertaining to the issue of I.D. documents, but these differences are for the most part little more than variations on a theme. One can apply sound, basic principles to any number of particular areas. This is especially the case when the countries fall into some kind of general category, such as the Commonwealth countries of England, Australia, and New Zealand. Although similar in many respects to the United States, Canada is included here because it, too, is a major Commonwealth country and is often excluded from I.D. manuals dealing primarily with the United States. Reciprocal and bilateral agreements between the above-noted countries, as well as others, regarding travel and employment mean that there are many advantages to be had by holding valid I.D. issued by Commonwealth nations. Whenever possible, samples of actual application forms have been included so that you may see *exactly* what the different requirements are.

FAKE I.D.

In England and Australia, and to a limited extent in the other countries covered herein, fake I.D. is often offered for sale to naive souls in search of a fresh start. The buyers are usually from out of state or are out-of-country immigrants who do not even know what the genuine document should look like. As a result, such people try to pass the most obvious of fake documents, ensuring that their liberty is rapidly curtailed. Not a very good start to a new life.

The only safe way to secure new I.D. is to get it yourself through legitimate channels.

GENUINE I.D.

Having warned you of the perils of fake I.D., it is worth pointing out that the systems of issue for I.D. documents in England are so sloppy and decentralized that obtaining genuine identification under various pretenses is easy.

It is possible—indeed, it is quite common—for a person to arrive in England armed only with suitable motivation, a passable English accent, and a set of good excuses to obtain various identification documents in remarkably short order. Such a person could either continue on his or her merry way to another country using his new identity, or start a new life in England.

So easy is it to obtain new I.D. in England, that the "clean-slater" might do well to consider commencing a new life as a citizen of England. Loopholes exist there which help to grease the wheels of an identification change, and it will be some time before they are closed. Combine these loopholes with the established practices of those who issue such documents—practices which are fine in a world of caring, honest people, but totally unsuited for the real one—and one has a situation that makes changing an identity as simple as changing socks.

1. ENGLAND

Of all the I.D. one can obtain in England, the single most important document—apart from a passport—is a full driver's license.

OBTAINING A DRIVER'S LICENSE

Because a full driver's license is acceptable identification for a wide range of purposes, it is the most common form of I.D. requested by police or other law-enforcement agencies. At the time of this writing, it will cost you £10 in cash, and may take as long as six months (the average waiting time for taking the driving test) to obtain such a license.

Before one can apply for a driving test, however, it is necessary to obtain what is known in England as a *provisional* license. This document allows the holder to drive vehicles on the highway provided he or she is accompanied by a qualified driver (one who has passed the driving test). The vehicle being driven must also display "L" plates to alert other drivers to the fact that an inexperienced motorist is on the move!

Obtaining the provisional license is a simple matter of completing the application form—available from any large post office—and sending it, along with the fee, to the Driver and Vehicle Licensing Centre, Swansea, SA99 1AD.

No checks are made of the applicants, no supporting documents are required, and no photographs are needed. Neither the provisional license nor the full license has photographs of the holder, leading to widespread abuse of the document.

It can often take more than a month before the provisional license is sent to the applicant. This delay is due to the work volume at the DVLC and does not indicate that any cross-referencing is being undertaken. The following pages show a current license application form, which is self-explanatory and provides all the information you will need.

Reciprocal Agreements

The possession of a full British license entitles the holder to request from the relevant authority a license issued by any other European Economic Community (EEC) country as well as most of the Commonwealth countries. Similarly, the holder of a full license issued in another member country can request a full British license.

Driving Test

While you are waiting for the provisional license to be sent to you, you can prepare for the driving test.

In Britain, the driving test consists of an eye test in which you must be able to read a standard vehicle number plate in good daylight, at a distance of sixty-seven feet. This distance is for plates with figures three inches high. (I have spent considerable time in England, and I have never seen what one could honestly call "good daylight," so I wouldn't bother too much about this requirement. All you really need is average eyesight.)

The driving portion of the test is easy, round-the-town stuff. You will have to reverse around a corner, and complete a three-point turn and emergency stop. You will have plenty of practice at this latter maneuver as you and fifty other learners battle for road space with crazed cabbies and half-blind bus drivers!

Following the actual driving, you will be tested on your knowledge of the various road signs. If you are not used to British driving, I suggest you pick up a copy of the "Highway Code" as soon as you arrive in England. This book will explain everything you might be asked on the test and is well worth studying. If you pass the driving test, the examiner will tell you then and there and give you a pass certificate. You must then complete Form D1, shown below, and send it to the DVLC. Enclose the pass certificate but not the provisional license. (The form explains the procedure.)

DVLC

Application for Your Driving Licence

Please do not write above this line

Please complete this form in **BLACK INK** and **BLOCK LETTERS**

If you need more information before you fill in this form please ask at your post office for leaflet D100.

To drive a Heavy Goods Vehicle or a Public Service Vehicle you need an additional licence. Consult a Traffic Area Office.

Address
You must give an address in England, Scotland or Wales where you live permanently. If you cannot do this, give the name and address of a person who does live there and through whom we may contact you at any time.

Types of Licence

- **Provisional licence** (1 and 2)
  This allows you to drive motor vehicles with a view to passing a driving test. You will not need a provisional licence if you hold a full licence which gives cover to drive, as a learner, other groups of vehicles.
  If you are applying for your first provisional licence do not drive until you receive it.
  IMPORTANT
  If you wish to ride a MOTOR-CYCLE as a learner now or when you reach age 17 you MUST tick the Provisional Box 2. The term motorcycle includes scooter but not moped. If you are under 17 and ask for motorcycle entitlement it will start from your 17th birthday.

- **Full licence** (3)
  You may apply for a full licence if during the last 10 years you have:
  - passed the British driving test; or
  - held a British full licence; or
  - held a full licence issued in Northern Ireland, the Channel Islands or the Isle of Man
  or if you hold:
  - a valid licence issued by a country recognised for exchange purposes (this covers all member states of the European Economic Community including a British Forces Germany licence) and you apply within one year of becoming resident in the United Kingdom.
  Otherwise you may only apply for provisional entitlement.

- **Duplicate licence** (4)
  To replace a lost, stolen, destroyed or defaced licence.

- **Exchange licence** (5)
  For a driver:
  - who holds a current full GB licence and wants new group(s) added to it; or
  - whose existing licence contains out of date endorsements (see leaflet D100); or
  - who wants provisional motorcycle entitlement added to the licence (see leaflet D100); or
  - who wishes to 'give up' provisional motorcycle entitlement—(see leaflet D100).
  An exchange licence will normally expire on the same date as the licence being exchanged.

Department of Transport

1 About yourself

a. Surname
   Christian or forenames

   Please tick box or state other title such as Dr. Rev.

b. Mr [1]   Mrs [2]   Miss [3]
   Other title

   Your full permanent address in Great Britain (see note on left)

c. Number and Road
   District or Village
   Post Town
   Postcode (Your licence may be delayed if the postcode is not quoted)

d. Please tick box   Male [1]   Female [2]

e. Please give your date of birth   Day Month Year

f. Have you ever held a British licence (full or provisional)? Answer **YES or NO**
   If YES please enter your Driver Number (if known) in the box below (and make a separate note of it).

2 What licence do you want?

a. Please tick the type of licence you want (see note 'Types of Licence' on left, especially the one headed IMPORTANT under Provisional licence)

   1 Provisional WITHOUT motorcycle entitlement
   2 Provisional WITH motorcycle entitlement
   3 Full   4 Duplicate   5 Exchange

b. When do you want your new licence to begin?   Day Month Year
   **A licence cannot be backdated.
   You can apply during the 2 months before you want your licence to begin.**

c. If you have passed a driving test since the issue of your last licence write the new Group passed here and enclose the pass certificate.

3 What was on your last licence?

Please ENCLOSE and give details of your last GB licence or any foreign licence you wish to exchange. All EEC licences will be returned to the issuing authority

a. If your last licence was surrendered on disqualification write S/D or if you have not previously held a GB licence, write NONE

b. Type of licence i.e. Provisional or Full

c. Expiry date

d. If your last licence has been lost, stolen, destroyed or defaced please tick the appropriate box below. If a lost licence is later found and is still current you must return it to DVLC.

   Lost or stolen [ ]   Destroyed [ ]   Defaced and I enclose it [ ]

e. Name and/or address on licence **if different from that at 1 above**
   Surname
   Christian or forenames
   Address
   Postcode (please quote)

Now please turn over
PRINTED IN THE U.K. FOR HMSO Dd8808941 7/84 AWO Ltd 00049

For DVLC use
Provisional-1   Rec. type
Full-2
Cont. No.

MC
DRE   End
Iss No.
TPC
Ent.

MP   RE   VDOB
MIM   Amount
DAM

Form D1: Application for an English driver's license.

List for question 4b
- Driving or attempting to drive while under the influence of drink or drugs.
- Driving or attempting to drive with an excess of alcohol in the body.
- Failure to provide a specimen of breath, blood or urine at a police station after driving or attempting to drive a motor vehicle.
- Aiding or abetting one of the above offences.

Health
See also section on Physical and Mental Fitness in leaflet D100. Among the reasons for answering **YES** to 6e and for giving details are:
- that you have been treated for drug addiction in the last three years; or
- that you have diabetes; or
- that you have a heart condition or are fitted with a cardiac pacemaker.

If you have or have had epilepsy, you may still be considered for a licence if you have been free from attacks for two years; or if you have attacks only while asleep, you must have established a pattern of such attacks over a period of more than three years.

Fees
Provisional licence
- First provisional licence £10
- Renewal of provisional licence issued before 1.10.82 £10 (Free for future renewals)

Full licence
- First GB full licence £10 (Free if you have already paid £10 for your provisional licence). Renewal of full licence if last full licence was:
  - Issued before 1.1.76 £10 (Free for future renewals)
  - Issued after 1.1.76 not being an exchange licence and no additional entitlement claimed. FREE

Duplicate licence £3

Exchange licence £3

How to pay
Please do not send cash or banknotes unless you have to and then only use Registered Post.

Cheques or postal orders should be made payable to 'Department of Transport' and crossed 'Motor Tax Account'. Post-dated cheques cannot be accepted. Please write your name and address on the back of any cheque. If you are paying by National Girobank transfer write 'Driving Licence Account' in the space provided for the number of the account to be credited. **The transfer form must be sent to the Driver and Vehicle Licensing Centre with the application.**

IMPORTANT NOTES
Driving without a licence
The law allows you to drive even if you do not actually have a licence provided that:
- you have held a licence before and are still entitled to obtain one (that is you are not disqualified or the licence would not be or has not been refused on medical grounds);
- a valid application for a licence has been received at the Driver and Vehicle Licensing Centre; and
- you can meet any conditions which apply when using that licence, such as those applicable to provisional licence holders.

You can drive without actually holding a licence for only one year from the date of receipt of the application by the DVLC.

Enquiries about your licence
To allow for time in the post to and from the Centre, please allow **at least 3 weeks** for your licence to arrive. If you do not receive it by then, please contact the Driver Enquiry Unit, DVLC, Swansea SA6 7JL, or telephone: 0792-72151 quoting your Driver Number or your full names and date of birth.

Your licence may be delayed if you do not answer ALL the questions

4 Driving offences
a. Are you disqualified by a Court from holding or obtaining a driving licence? _____

Answer **YES** or **NO** [ ] If **YES** give date and period of disqualification _____

Court _____

b. Has a Court ordered you to be disqualified or your licence to be endorsed for **ANY** offence in the last **4** years (or in the last **11** years for any offence in the list on the left)?

Answer **YES** or **NO** [ ] If **YES** give details of all disqualifications and endorsements

Date of conviction _____ Court _____

Offence _____

Date of conviction _____ Court _____

Offence _____

If necessary state other disqualifications/endorsements (or details of successful appeals) on a separate sheet; date it, sign it and enclose it with this application.

If you enclose a separate sheet please tick box [ ]

5 Your eyesight
Can you read a vehicle number plate in good daylight (with glasses if worn), at 67 feet for figures 3⅛" high?

Answer **YES** or **NO** _____ (If **NO** you may still be able to obtain a licence for a pedestrian controlled vehicle or a mowing machine – see leaflet D100).

6 Your health
Questions 6a–6e **MUST** be answered (Please do not use a tick or dash)

a. Have you ever had a licence refused or revoked for medical reasons?

Answer **YES** or **NO** [ ] If **YES** give date and reasons _____

If you are in doubt about your answers to 6b, 6c, 6d or 6e consult your doctor

b. Has a doctor ever advised you not to drive?

Answer **YES** or **NO** [ ] If **YES** give details _____

c. Are you without hand or foot or have you any defect in limb movement or power?

Answer **YES** or **NO** [ ] If **YES** give details _____

If the answer is **YES** and you have held a licence before
(i) was this limb disability mentioned in your previous application? Answer **YES** or **NO** [ ]
(ii) If so, has it got worse since then? Answer **YES** or **NO** _____ [ ]

d. Have you now or have you ever had epilepsy or sudden attacks of disabling giddiness or fainting or any mental illness or defect?

Answer **YES** or **NO** [ ] If **YES** give details _____

e. Have you now or have you ever had any other disability or medical condition which could affect your fitness as a driver either now or in the future? (see 'Health' note on the left)

Answer **YES** or **NO** [ ] If **YES** give details _____

7 Your declaration
Warning: If you or anyone else knowingly gives false information to help you obtain this licence, you and they are liable to prosecution.

I apply for a driving licence

I enclose the fee of £ _____ (if applicable, see notes on the left) Postal Order/Cheque no. _____

I declare that I have checked the details I have given and that to the best of my knowledge they are correct, and that I am entitled to the licence for which I am applying.

Your Signature _____ Date _____

- If you are enclosing an EEC licence which entitles you to drive heavy goods (HGV) or public service (PSV) vehicles and you wish to drive any such vehicles in Great Britain you will need a GB HGV or PSV licence. Please tick this box [ ] and make a separate application as soon as possible to the Traffic Area Office in which area you live.

| If you are applying for your FIRST British licence, please send this form to:– First Application Section, DVLC, SWANSEA SA99 1AD | RENEWAL, Duplicate and Exchange applications should be sent to:– Driver Licence Section, DVLC, SWANSEA SA99 1AB |

✗ Please remember to enclose your last licence, fee and test pass certificate, if applicable.

Driving Test Application Form

An English driving test application form is shown on the following pages. By reading it carefully, you will be able to determine what type of license you require. The form also details what the applicant must be able to do in order to pass the test, depending on the type of vehicle used.

The form makes the whole thing sound a lot more complicated than it really is. There is a saying in England that goes something like, "you are not learning to drive, but rather to pass the test." Consider this saying, especially if you have already been driving for some time. Keep in mind that you are supposed to be a novice; you are therefore not expected to drive as aggressively or confidently as a seasoned motorist. To do so would not really make an examiner in England suspicious, but it may well annoy him and adversely affect your chances of passing. Displaying a lot of respect and courtesy—toward the examiner and other motorists—is a guarantee of success, providing you can actually operate the vehicle!

As you complete the form, pay particular attention to questions 7 to 10. If you are in a hurry to obtain a new license, it is in your best interest to provide answers which indicate your immediate availability and readiness to take the test—any time of the day or week. There is a considerable waiting list for test applicants—in some parts of the country as long as six months—so it is important you give yourself a head start over those that have specified certain times of the day or days of the week.

Notice that the fee for the test is not indicated on the application form, the reason being that the fee changes from time to time and reprinting the forms would be a waste of money and effort. The fee current at the time of applying for the test is displayed in major post offices and driving-test centers. Make a note of it when you collect an application form.

NATIONAL INSURANCE NUMBER CARD

One would suspect that the National Insurance number (also known as the Social Security number) would be the most important identification in the British pocket. After all, possession of such a number enables the holder to draw unemployment benefits and a variety of other state handouts. However, the majority of British people do not know their N.I. number off hand, and only a small percentage of the population ever gets an "official" National Insurance number card.

The reasons for this are complex, but it is possible to summarize them by explaining that in normal, everyday life, there is no demand for the British citizen to know his number. In employment, the relevant information pertaining to a person's insurance number is sent out once a year on tax forms and the like. At the commencement of unemployment, a person gives the required information (N.I. number, for example) and the number is not usually called for again. Even if he or she does not know the number, it is assumed that it will be found "somewhere in the system." A name and date of birth are, of course, required.

The easiest way to obtain a genuine National Insurance number is to go to a local Social Security office (as numerous as pubs in England today) and ask for one. Your only requirement is a suitable excuse for not having one!

The most often used excuse given by a person seeking a number is that he has been living and working with a traveling circus or fair since his childhood. Therefore, he has never paid any tax, having just learned to read and write properly. Realizing that he is not registered anywhere—and having been told that he should be—he has come to the office to seek advice.

The office staff will ask plenty of questions, but if you have prepared your answers properly—ensuring that they cannot be *disproven*—you will be given a N.I. number on the spot, or at least within the next few days. It is important, of course, to convey the correct image: Do not go to the office dressed in a new suit and speaking with an accent used by members of the upper class. In fact, the more stupid and uneducated you appear, the better. If you can get someone to go to the office with you and explain that you are a bit slow, not very bright, and need help to understand the forms, so much the better.

A degree of acting ability is called for in order to successfully execute this technique. On a busy day, though, an overworked assistant will be only too pleased to pigeonhole you as soon as possible.

An important aspect of this method is that you do not give the impression you are after money. (Many people only bother to register at such offices because they are broke.) If you seem to be a simple, confused idiot who is only there because

Department of Transport

Road Traffic Act 1972
The Motor Vehicles (Driving Licences) Regulations 1981 and
The Motor Vehicles (Driving Licences) (Amendment) Regulations 1982

Application for a driving test appointment

Details of the Driving Test including Part II for Motor Bicycles

> If you have not read the pamphlet:
> **Your driving test (DL68)**
> **please do so**
>
> A copy of this pamphlet may be obtained free from your Traffic Area Office (see page 4)

The Regulations require an applicant for a driving licence to satisfy the Examiner: that he is fully conversant with the contents of the Highway Code; and generally, that he is competent to drive without danger to and with due consideration for other users of the road, a vehicle of the same class or description as that on which he is tested. In addition, the candidate must fulfil the requirements at items 1 to 6, and such of the additional requirements at items 7 to 12 in relation to the Group of vehicles which includes the one on which the test is taken as are specified in the Table below.

1. Read in good daylight (with the aid of glasses if worn) a registration mark fixed to a motor vehicle at a distance of 75 feet in the case of a registration mark containing letters and figures 3½ inches high or at a distance of 67 feet in the case of a registration mark containing letters and figures 3⅛ inches high. (In the case of a test taken on a Group K vehicle only, the reading distances are 45 feet for the larger registration mark and 40 feet for the smaller size.)
2. Start the engine of the vehicle.
3. Move away straight ahead or at an angle;
4. Overtake, meet or cross the path of other vehicles and take an appropriate course;
5. Turn right-hand and left-hand corners correctly;
6. Stop the vehicle in an emergency and normally, and in the latter case bring it to rest at an appropriate part of the road;
7. Drive the vehicle backwards and whilst so doing enter a limited opening either to the right or left;
8. Cause the vehicle to face in the opposite direction by the use of forward and reverse gears;
9. Indicate his intended actions at appropriate times by giving appropriate signals in a clear and unmistakable manner;
10. Act correctly and promptly on all signals given by traffic signs and traffic controllers and take appropriate action on signs given by other road users;
11. Drive the vehicle backwards and cause it to face in the opposite direction by means of its tracks;
12. Passed Part I of the test for motor bicycles, (except for residents of islands not connected to the mainland of Great Britain by a crossing suitable for motor vehicles, other than the Isle of Wight, Lewis and Harris, North Uist, Benbecula and South Uist, Mainland Orkney, Mainland Shetland and Skye and islands connected to these named islands by a crossing suitable for motor vehicles).

Details of Part I of the motor bicycle driving test for motor bicycles without side-cars

The Regulations provide for a two-part driving test for riders of motor bicycles (without side-cars). Part I requires such riders to execute the following manoeuvres competently to the satisfaction of the person conducting the test.
Drive the vehicle round a predetermined left-hand circuit bringing it to rest when signalled to do so.
Drive the vehicle round a predetermined right-hand circuit bringing it to rest when signalled to do so.
Drive the vehicle round a predetermined right-hand circuit bringing it to rest at a predetermined point.
Drive the vehicle straight ahead to reach a speed of approximately 15 miles per hour, bringing it to rest at a predetermined point.
Drive the vehicle in and out of a line of markers on a predetermined course, bringing it to rest when signalled to do so.
Drive the vehicle round a figure-of-eight circuit bringing it to rest when signalled to do so.
Drive the vehicle slowly while keeping alongside the person conducting the test as he walks at a varying pace until signalled to stop.

Table of vehicle groups

If you pass a test (which, for solo motorcyclists, means both Parts I and II of the motor bicycle driving test) you will be entitled to drive any vehicle in the Group including the vehicle on which you were tested and any vehicle in any Group(s) shown in the fourth column, opposite that Group. If therefore, you want to drive, say, a motor car and an agricultural tractor, you should take a test on a vehicle in Group A or Group B. Separate tests are necessary for HGV and PSV drivers' licences. You do not need a licence or to take a test for a pedestrian controlled mowing machine.

Group	Class or description of vehicle included in the group	Additional requirements (see details of driving test above)	Additional groups covered
A	A vehicle without automatic transmission, of any class not included in any other group	7, 8, 9 and 10	B, C, E, F, K and L
B	A vehicle with automatic transmission, of any class not included in any other group	7, 8, 9 and 10	E, F, K and L
C	Motor tricycle weighing not more than 425 kg unladen, but excluding any vehicle included in group E, J, K or L.	9 and 10 and if fitted with a means of reversing 7 and 8	E, K and L
D	Motor bicycle (with or without side-car), but excluding any vehicle included in group E, K or L.	9, 10 and, if a motor bicycle without side-car, 12	C, E and motor cycles in group L
E	Moped	9 and 10	—
F	Agricultural tractor, but excluding any vehicle included in group H	7, 9 and 10	K
G	Road roller	7, 9 and 10	—
H	Track-laying vehicle steered by its tracks	9, 10 and 11	—
J	Invalid carriage	9 and 10	—
K	Mowing machine or pedestrian controlled vehicle	None	—
L	Vehicle propelled by electrical power, but excluding any vehicle included in group E, J or K	9 and 10 and if fitted with a means of reversing 7 and 8	K
M	—	—	—
N	Vehicle exempted from duty under section 7(1) of the Vehicles (Excise) Act 1971	None	—

GENERAL NOTES Please read the notes and the questions on page 2 carefully before writing your answers on page 3.

FEES – The fee for a test appointment is displayed in all Driving Test Centres, Traffic Area Offices, Local Vehicle Licensing Offices and DVLC Swansea (Tel No 0792 72151), or you may telephone any Traffic Area Office (Tel Nos on page 4), and Ansaphone service for London Tel No 01-743 2087 and Edinburgh Tel No 031-228 6062). A poster is also displayed in all Crown Post Offices for 3 months after a fee increase. No fee is payable for a test with an invalid carriage.

DRIVING LICENCE – If you are in possession of your driving licence or driving permit at the time of your test, please bring it with you.

SOLO MOTORCYCLISTS – **If you are applying for Part II of the test you must enclose your Certificate of Passing Part I (form DL23MC).** If you have lost your Certificate a duplicate may be obtained from either the appointed training organisation, if you took Part I of the test with that organisation, or, if you took your test at a Deparment of Transport Heavy Goods Vehicle driving test centre, from the Clerk at the Traffic Area Office for the Area in which Part I of the test was conducted.

DL26 (Rev 12/83)

Driving test appointment application.

PENALTY – AN APPLICANT WHO, FOR THE PURPOSE OF OBTAINING A LICENCE, KNOWINGLY MAKES A FALSE STATEMENT IS LIABLE TO A FINE NOT EXCEEDING £500.

Explanatory notes: *Please write answers on page 3 opposite.*

1 **Name** – give your first Christian or other name and surname in full; for the rest of your Christian or other names, give initials only. Delete the titles Mr, Mrs, Miss or Ms which do **NOT** apply. USE BLOCK LETTERS PLEASE.

2 **Address** – your full postal address including postcode. USE BLOCK LETTERS PLEASE. *If you change your address you should inform the Traffic Area Office to which you send this application, to enable them to contact you if your appointment has to be altered for any reason.*

3 **Telephone number(s) (if any)**

4 **Centre** – a list of centres at which tests are normally conducted is on page 4. *Part I of the motor bicycle test will take place at Heavy Goods Vehicle driving test centres.* Insert the name of the centre at which you wish to be tested. Give an alternative centre if possible. For centres other than HGV centres within the Metropolitan Traffic Area insert the centre code.
EXAMPLE: For Hendon insert **HE**.
IMPORTANT: If you are a solo motorcyclist applying for Part I of the test also tick the space provided.

5 **Type of vehicle** – you must supply a suitable vehicle for the test. It must not be loaded or partially loaded and the examiner must be able to take observation through the rear of the vehicle. State the type of vehicle to be used. The following are examples: motor car, solo motor bicycle, motor bicycle with side-car, moped, motor tricycle, commercial vehicle other than a heavy goods vehicle, road roller, agricultural tractor, invalid carriage, pedestrian controlled vehicle. If you are a solo motorcyclist, state engine capacity of machine.

6 **Details of previous test** – if you have had a previous test for a vehicle within the same group please give place and date. If you are a solo motorcyclist applying for Part I of the motor bicycle test, do **not** answer this question.

7 **Earliest date** – give the earliest DATE from which you will be available for a test. Please answer specifically: do not answer "As soon as possible." With the exception of Part I of the motor bicycle test you are ineligible to take a driving test within one calendar month of a previous test on a vehicle within the same group. Your answer must take account of any such limitation. Do not come forward for your driving test until you and your instructor are confident you are fully prepared.

8 **Unacceptable days of the week** – put a cross in the appropriate box for any day or half day on which you could **NOT** take a test. For the whole day put a cross in both *am* and *pm* boxes. The less you cross out the better chance you will have of an earlier test date.

9 **Unacceptable dates** – give details of any periods (eg holidays) and/or single dates **after the date given in answer to question 7 when you will NOT** be available to take a test. Indicate whether the dates given are periods or separate dates.

10 **Test at short notice** – could you accept an appointment at short notice (less than a week) if one is available? Tick **yes** or **no**.

11 **Disabilities** – state physical disabilities. If none, state **"NONE."**

12 **Driving Schools** – if you are with a driving school insert name and telephone number of school: In the Metropolitan Traffic Area ask your school to insert their code number in the box marked driving school code.

13 **Complete the application giving details of fee enclosed and cheque or postal order number.**
BANK NOTES AND COINS MUST NOT BE SENT. Cheques and postal orders should be made payable to the Department of Transport and crossed /& Co/. If you use a cheque write your name, address and choice of centre(s) on the back. If you use a postal order fill in and retain the counterfoil until you have received an appointment card.

14 **Driver number** – copied from the top of your driving licence.

15 *Please make sure you sign the form.*

When you have answered all the questions please detach page 3 of the form and send it with your fee to the Clerk at the Traffic Area Office for your Area, at the address given on page 4.

If you are applying for Part II of the motor bicycle test enclose your Certificate of passing Part I

IN DUE COURSE you will receive a card giving you details of your test appointment. If you have not received this card within 21 days you should inform the Traffic Area Office (Driving Tests) at the address to which you sent the application.

Application for a driving test appointment

Answers BLOCK LETTERS PLEASE AND WRITE CLEARLY IN INK

For official use only: do not write in the spaces below

1 Surname

Mr / Mrs / Miss / Ms | First Christian or other name | Other initials

2 T   3 Initials

2 Address
- Line 1
- Line 2
- Line 3
- Line 4   Postcode

3 Telephone Number(s) — Home / Work

DL 23MC Noted
Cert. No. ....
Date Returned to Candidate
........................198......

4 Centre
- 1st Choice
- 2nd Choice
- Part I motor bicycle test   Yes ☐

5 Type of vehicle

8 V/T   P

6 Previous test   Place   Date

7 Earliest date

9 D   M

8 Unacceptable day(s) of the week

Monday	Tuesday	Wednesday	Thursday	Friday
am pm	am pm	am pm	am pm	am pm
1 2	3 4	5 6	7 8	9 0

10

11 ind   D   M   D   M

9 Unacceptable dates

12 S/N

10 Test at short notice   Yes ☐   No ☐

Dis

11 Disabilities

12 Name of driving school
Telephone number

13   Driving school code

13 Fee enclosed
£ _____   Cheque No or Postal Order No

14 D   M   P

14 Driver number

15 Usual signature of applicant   Date

← PLEASE WRITE YOUR NAME AND ADDRESS HERE IN BLOCK LETTERS

READ STUDY PRACTICE THE HIGHWAY CODE

TRAFFIC AREA OFFICE

DRIVING TEST CENTRES

Notes: At centres shown in italics tests are conducted only on certain weekdays
Part I motor bicycle tests are conducted from Heavy Goods Vehicle Centres (shown in bold type) on certain weekdays.

NORTH EASTERN TRAFFIC AREA
(Newcastle)
Westgate House, Westgate Road
Newcastle-upon-Tyne, NE1 1TW
(Tel No 610031)

Alnwick, Berwick-on-Tweed, Bishop Auckland, Blyth, Darlington, Durham, Gateshead, Gosforth, Hartlepool, Hexham, Jarrow, Longbenton, Middlesbrough, Newcastle-upon-Tyne, Northallerton, North Shields, Redcar, Sunderland, Thornaby.

Part I motor bicycle tests – **Berwick, Darlington, Newcastle.**

NORTH EASTERN TRAFFIC AREA
(Leeds)
Hillcrest House
386 Harehills Lane, Leeds
LS9 6NF
(Tel No 495661)

Barnsley, Bradford (Eccleshill, Heaton and Wibsey), Bridlington, Cleethorpes, Doncaster, Goole, Grimsby, Halifax, Heckmondwike, Hessle, Harrogate, Horsforth, Huddersfield, Hull (Park Street and Salisbury Street), Keighley, Leeds (Harehills and Crossgates), *Malton,* Pontefract, Rotherham, Scarborough, Scunthorpe, Sheffield (Handsworth, Middlewood Road and Manor Top), Skipton, Wakefield, *Whitby,* York.

Part I motor bicycle tests – **Beverley, Grimsby, Keighley, Leeds, Sheffield, Walton (York).**

NORTH WESTERN TRAFFIC AREA
Arkwright House
Parsonage Gardens
Deansgate, Manchester, M60 9AN
(Tel No Manchester 832 8644)

Bala, Bangor, Barrow, Birkenhead, Blackburn, Blackpool, Bolton, Bury, *Buxton,* Carlisle, Chester, Chorley, *Congleton,* Crewe, Ellesmere Port, Failsworth, Heysham, *Holyhead,* Hyde, Kendal, Liverpool (Bootle, Crosby, Garston and Norris Green), *Llandudno,* Macclesfield, Manchester (Cheetham Hill, Didsbury, Whalley Range and Withington), Mold, Northwich, Nelson, Preston, *Pwllheli, Reddish,* Rhyl, Rochdale, Sale, Southport, St. Helens, Wallasey, Warrington, Widnes, Wigan, Wilmslow, Workington, Wrexham.

Part I motor bicycle tests – **Bredbury (Manchester), Caernarfon, Carlisle, Heywood (Manchester), Kirkham (Preston), Simonswood (Liverpool), Wirral (Birkenhead), Wrexham.**

WEST MIDLAND TRAFFIC AREA
Cumberland House
200 Broad Street
Birmingham B15 1TD
(Tel No Birmingham 643 5011)

Bilston, Birmingham (Kings Heath, Kingstanding, Quinton, Sheldon and Washwood Heath), Bromsgrove, Burton-on-Trent, Cannock, Cobridge, Coventry (Mason Road and Holyhead Road), *Evesham,* Fenton, Hereford, Kidderminster, Leamington, *Leek,* Lichfield, Lower Gornal, *Ludlow, Malvern,* Newcastle-under-Lyme, Nuneaton, *Oswestry,* Redditch, Rugby, Shirley, Shrewsbury, Stafford, *Stratford-on-Avon,* Sutton Coldfield, Walsall (Bloxwich), Wednesbury, Wellington, *Whitchurch,* Wolverhampton, Worcester.

Part I motor bicycle tests – **Featherstone (Wolverhampton), Garretts Green (Birmingham), Shrewsbury, Swynnerton (Stoke on Trent).**

EASTERN TRAFFIC AREA
(Nottingham)
Birkbeck House
14-16 Trinity Square
Nottingham, NG1 4BA
(Tel No 475511)

Ashbourne, Boston, Chesterfield, Derby (Sinfin Lane and London Road), *Gainsborough,* Grantham, Hinckley, Kettering, Leicester (Gipsy Lane, Narborough Road and Welford Road), Lincoln, Loughborough, *Louth, Melton Mowbray, Newark,* Northampton, Nottingham (Arnold, Beeston, Chalfont Drive and West Bridgford), *Skegness,* Spalding, *Stamford,* Sutton-in-Ashfield, Wellingborough, Worksop.

Part I motor bicycle tests – **Alvaston (Derby), Leicester, Watnall (Nottingham), Weedon.**

EASTERN TRAFFIC AREA
(Cambridge)
Terrington House, 13-15 Hills Road
Cambridge, CB2 1NP
(Tel No 358922)

Bedford, Bury St Edmunds, Cambridge (Brooklands Avenue and Chesterton Road), Chelmsford, Clacton, Colchester, Ipswich, King's Lynn, Leighton Buzzard, Lowestoft, Luton, Norwich (Jupiter Road and Earlham House), Peterborough, Southend-on-Sea, Wisbech.

Part I motor bicycle tests – **Chelmsford, Ipswich, Leighton Buzzard, Norwich, Peterborough, Waterbeach (Cambridge).**

SOUTH WALES TRAFFIC AREA
Caradog House
1-6 St Andrew's Place
Cardiff, Glamorgan, CF1 3PW
(Tel No 0222 24801)

Abergavenney, Aberystwyth, Ammanford, *Barry, Brecon,* Bridgend, Cardiff (Cathays Terrace and Norbury Road), *Cardigan, Carmarthen,* Cwmbran, Haverfordwest, *Lampeter, Llandrindod Wells,* Llanelli, Machynlleth, Merthyr Tydfil, *Milford Haven, Monmouth,* Newport, *Newtown, Pembroke Dock,* Pontypridd, Swansea, *Treorchy.*

Part I motor bicycle tests – **Llantrisant, Neath, Pontypool, Templeton (Haverfordwest).**

WESTERN TRAFFIC AREA
The Gaunt's House
Denmark Street
Bristol, BS1 5DR
(Tel No 297221)

Barnstaple, Bath (Foxhill and Sydney Road), Bodmin, Bournemouth, Bridgwater, Bristol (Ashton Gate, Clifton Down, Southmead and St. George), Cheltenham, Chippenham, Devonport, Dorchester, Exeter, *Exmouth,* Gloucester, *Launceston, Minehead,* Newton Abbot, Penzance, Plymouth, Poole, Salisbury, *Scilly Isles,* Swindon, Taunton, *Tiverton,* Trowbridge, Truro, *Wells,* Weston-super-Mare, Yeovil.

Part I motor bicycle tests – **Bristol, Camborne, Chiseldon (Swindon), Exeter, Gloucester, Plymouth, Taunton.**

SOUTH EASTERN TRAFFIC AREA
Ivy House, 3 Ivy Terrace
Eastbourne, BN21 4QT
(Tel No 0323 21471)

Aldershot, Ashford (Kent), Aylesbury, Banbury, Basingstoke, Bletchley, Brighton, Canterbury, Caversham, Chichester, Crawley, Eastbourne, Farnborough, Folkestone, Gillingham, Gosport, Gravesend, Hastings, Henley-on-Thames, Herne Bay, High Wycombe, Hove, Maidstone, Margate, Newbury, Newport (IOW), Oxford (Headington and Marston Road), Portsmouth, Reading, Slough, Southampton (Forest Hills Drive and Maybush), Tunbridge Wells, Winchester, Witney, Worthing.

Part I motor bicycle tests – **Canterbury, Culham, Gillingham, Hastings, Isle of Wight, Lancing, Reading, Southampton.**

SCOTTISH TRAFFIC AREA
83 Princes Street
Edinburgh, EH2 2ER
(Tel No 031 225 5418)

Alloa, Ayr, Bathgate, *Callander,* Campbeltown, Castle Douglas, Coatbridge, *Cumnock,* Dumbarton, Dumfries, *Dunoon, Duns,* Edinburgh (Joppa, Newington and Parkhead), Falkirk, Galashiels, *Girvan,* Glasgow (Anniesland, Riddrie, Rutherglen, Shawlands, Shettleston), Greenock, *Haddington,* Hamilton, Hawick, Inveraray, Kelso, Kilmarnock, Lanark, Lochgilphead, Newton Stewart, *Oban,* Paisley, Peebles, *Rothesay,* Saltcoats, Stirling, Stranraer, *Tighnabruaich,* Wishaw. ISLANDS: Brodick, Islay, Millport, Mull, Tiree.

Part I motor bicycle tests – **Bishopbriggs (Glasgow), Drem, Dumfries, Galashiels, Kilmarnock, Livingston (Edinburgh), Oban.**

Aberdeen (Albert Street and Clunie Place), *Aberfeldy,* Arbroath, *Ballachulish, Ballater,* Banff, Bettyhill, Blairgowrie, Brechin, *Buckie, Crieff, Cupar, Dingwall,* Dundee, Dunfermline, Elgin, Forfar, Fort Augustus, Fort William, Fraserburgh, *Gairloch, Golspie, Grantown-on-Spey, Helmsdale,* Huntly, Inverness, *Inverurie,* Keith, Kingussie, Kinross, Kirkcaldy, Kyle of Lochalsh, *Lairg, Lochinver, Mallaig, Montrose,* Perth, Peterhead, *Pitlochry,* Stonehaven, *Strontian, Tain,* Thurso, Turriff, Ullapool, Wick. ISLANDS: *Barra, Benbecula, Harris, Lewis,* North Uist, Orkney, Shetland, Skye, South Uist.

Part I motor bicycle tests – **Aberdeen, Elgin (Keith), Inverness, Kirkwall, Lerwick, Montrose, Perth, Stornoway, Wick.**

METROPOLITAN TRAFFIC AREA
PO Box 643
Government Buildings
Bromyard Avenue
The Vale, Acton, W3 7AY
(Tel No 01-743 5522)

Ashford (Surrey)	AS	Greenford		Morden	MO	Surbiton	SB
Barking	BG	(Horsenden Lane)	GN	Norwood	ND	Sutton	SN
Barnet	BT	(Ruislip Road)	GR	Palmers Green	PG	Teddington	TD
Belvedere	BE	Guildford	GF	Pinner	PI	Wallington (Wallington Court)	WL
Berkhamsted	BD	Hayes (Middx)	HA	Redhill	RL	(Old Town Hall)	WO
Bexleyheath	BX	Hendon	HE	Rickmansworth	RM	Wanstead	WS
Bishops Stortford	BS	Hitchin	HC	Ruislip	RP	Watford	WR
Brentwood	BW	Hither Green	HN	St Albans	SA	Wealdstone	WE
Burnt Oak	BK	Hornchurch	HU	Sevenoaks	SV	West Wickham	WW
Chertsey	CS	Ilford	IL	Sidcup	SP	Weybridge	WY
Chingford	CG	Isleworth	IS	Southall	SX	Winchmore Hill	WH
Croydon	CD	Lee	LE	Southfields	SF	Wood Green	
East Ham	EH	Loughton	LO	Southgate	SG	(Bounds Green Road)	WG
Grays	GY	Mill Hill	MH	Stevenage	ST	(Lordship Lane)	WN

Printed in the UK for HMSO
Dd. 8300924 2/84.

Part I motor bicycle tests – **Croydon, Enfield, Guildford, Purfleet, Yeading.**

someone told you you were supposed to have insurance numbers and the like, you are three quarters of the way toward victory.

The excuse for not having a number, not having worked "on the cards,"* should be credible. The following explanation is the best to use if you can present the correct image. Apply for registration at any local office as an unemployed person. When asked your National Insurance number, explain (in your best accent) that you were born in Eire (Republic of Ireland) and that you came to England to work. Make up a year for your arrival in England. Explain how you have worked on a casual basis—on building sites or farms, for example—and have never had the need to register as unemployed before. It never occurred to you, of course, to bother about insurance or such things.

You can pick a county name from any map of Eire, and make up the name of a farm, school, etc., depending on the questions you are asked. There is little, if any, cooperation between the English and Eire government departments, and the chances of anyone being able to disprove your story are quite remote. (An hour of drinking with an Irish-born local will provide you with all the information you may need.)

I have seen such techniques employed on many occasions and heard about their continued use from scores of people. Never, in any of the instances described, was identification in a tangible form requested by the office staff. It cannot be denied, however, that being able to produce a driver's license or some lesser document (union card, electric bill) would add weight to your claim.

Incidentally, a union card can be obtained by joining the appropriate local union office. There are a small fee and various questions, but no checks or identification requirement. An electric or other service bill is simply obtained by spending some time in a rented apartment and arranging for the services to be connected in your (new) name.

Once you have obtained a National Insurance number, you are well on the way to securing other documents. You will also be able to obtain legal employment in England and other EEC countries that have a reciprocal agreement with Britain.

---

*This is an English expression meaning to work legally—paying insurance contributions, income tax, and so on. Many people work "off the cards," meaning they work on a casual basis and do not declare their earnings to the state.

P45

If you begin working for an employer in England, you will be asked for P45—details of your personal income tax. Everybody who has ever worked legally (paid tax) will have one of these—however out of date it may be.

To obtain this document, tell your new employer that you have not worked on the cards for some time and that you have lost your old P45. He will then set the wheels in motion for the issue of a new one by contacting the tax office on your behalf. In the meantime, your wages will be taxed on an emergency basis. The amount that is deducted will be ridiculously high, but as a means to an end—the possession of a valid document—it will be well worth the expense.

In due course, a new P45 will be issued, and the tax office will send you a tax return form to complete and return. They will then assess your tax status and send you the details. In most cases, the tax office will ask you to explain what you have been doing for the past five years—where you have been working, why you have not paid tax, and so on. Do not take these questions too seriously. British tax-return forms rank high among the world's most intimidating paperwork, but it is all a bluff. Stick to your chosen story, and the tax office is unlikely to bother you again (well, not until next year, anyway).

OBTAINING A BIRTH CERTIFICATE

There are several ways in which one can obtain a birth certificate, and thereby adopt a different identity. However, not all of the methods work equally well in different countries, or even different areas of the same country, due to variations in local bylaws, different attitudes among issuing staff, and the volume of the work load at the various government offices.

Some covert research should be undertaken in order to determine the existing circumstances in a particular area before you seek a new certificate. Time and effort invested in this aspect of the project will be well repaid in the long run.

Selecting an Identity

The first technique we will discuss is known in England as *ghosting,* which, as its name implies, involves taking over where a dead person "left off." The first requirement is a suitable identity to adopt, and suitability is really only governed by nationality, sex and—more importantly—age. The age of the candiate at his or her death should be as young as possible—under the high-school graduating age, or preferable elementary-school age.

The reasons for this are twofold. Firstly, such a young person would not have generated any major records; therefore your new I.D. will be clean. Secondly, recent innovations such as marking birth certificates "died" in order to deter "ghosts" may not have been applied to the records of persons who had died prior to the adoption of the new system.

Needless to say, it is imperative that the age of the person, were he still living, should be within a couple of years of your own apparent age. I say apparent, because if you are really thirty-five but only look twenty-five, it might be safer to go for a certificate indicating an age nearer your true appearance.

Be honest, however, and don't be tempted to lose a few years for the sake of vanity!

The time-tested method of finding a suitable candidate is to search the tombstones of graveyards. This technique, or the less physical one of examining newspaper obituary columns available at all main city libraries, will provide many possibilities.

Applying for a birth certificate

Once you have selected an identity you consider suitable, your next consideration is to apply at the local registry office for a duplicate birth certificate. There is a small fee for this service, but since the amount of the fee varies, it is not given here.

The clerk at the office will ask for any information that you can supply regarding birth details. If, however, you are applying at the office responsible for storing details of the original birth information, only minimal details are required. For example, if the person was born in London, in the borough of Wadley, then the Wadley registry office is the place to apply. It is possible to obtain certificates from offices in other areas, but to do so entails additional effort on the part of the office staff (cross-referencing, for example) and you will probably have to return at a later date for the certificate. If you apply at the correct area office, you will be issued the document on the spot.

Depending on the attitude of the staff at the office at which you apply, you *may* have to complete a very basic request form. There is no standardized request/application form in use in England at this time, and I have never come across an office that uses such a form. The usual practice is for the clerk to jot down any information needed as the applicant gives the details. You will have to supply the name of the person to whom the certificate relates, the place of birth, father's name, and the mother's maiden name. A certificate will still be issued even if you cannot give the mother's maiden name, although if the name of the person on the certificate is a common one, there will be a delay.

No supportive identification is requested, and no cross-referencing exists at this time. The best excuse for requiring the certificate (although you are unlikely to be asked except out of idle curiosity) is that you require the certificate for a passport application, medical insurance claim, or something similar. Explain that a friend or workmate asked you to get him or her the certificate as he is too busy to get it himself. The system in England is very easy to manipulate, and the majority of people who become unstuck using certificates obtained in such a way are usually illegal immigrants. On record is the case of an Asian-born male who was caught trying to cash a check using an I.D. bearing the name "Patrick Maloney." There may well be some Patrick Maloneys around who are Asian but, even so, such a person will attract more attention than a person with similar racial features bearing a more appropriate name.

MEDICAL CARD AND NUMBER

This document should not be confused with the National Insurance number. It has nothing at all to do with employment, but is instead issued to citizens of the United Kingdom who are entitled to treatment or care under the National Health Service. To all intents and purposes, anyone legally residing in England is entitled to free or heavily subsidized health care whether or not he is employed and regardless of how much he has contributed financially toward the system. (Everyone pays the same—more or less—for prescription medicines, dental treatment, etc., and emergency treatment is free.)

In theory, a medical card—which shows only the name and medical number of the holder—should be produced when seeking treatment from a doctor other than the one with which the patient is

CERTIFICATE OF BIRTH

1 & 2 ELIZ. 2 CH. 20

B. Cert. S.
R.B.D.

Name and Surname: ALAN ANYBODY

Sex: BOY

Date of Birth: 5th JANUARY 1959

Place of Birth:
- Registration District: LONDON
- Sub-district: WOLVERTON

I, Stephen Salisbury, Registrar of Births and Deaths for the Sub-district of .... HOSPITAL do hereby certify that the above particulars have been compiled from an entry in a register in my custody.

Witness my hand this 22nd day of October 1984.

CAUTION :—*Any person who (1) falsifies any of the particulars on this certificate, or (2) uses a falsified certificate as true, knowing it to be false, is liable to prosecution.*

S. Salisbury
Registrar of Births and Deaths

The birth certificate is used by most people in England for identification purposes. A full copy of the original certificate, showing details of parents, etc., can also be obtained. Note that photocopies of documents are *not* acceptable for official use in England.

registered. In practice, few people have a medical card in their possession. Fewer still can remember their number offhand. Therefore, the doctor will simply ask for the name and address of the doctor with whom the patient is registered and cross-check the details at a later date. This practice means that free or very cheap health care is available for anyone who cares to avail himself of the system!

There is no legal requirement for persons to register with a doctor, and many people do not do so until they become ill. However, for those of you seeking a new identity, registration is recommended. Doing so will entitle you to a medical card and number.

Any doctor who works for the National Health Service will be happy to accommodate you and issue a card if you approach him in the correct manner. (Explain you moved to England from Ireland some time ago and never bothered to register with a doctor because you never saw the need to do so.) Give the doctor any address and county name, which can be pulled from any map of Eire or an Irish directory, and the name you have chosen for yourself. You will, no doubt, be given a card and number on the spot.

NATIONAL HEALTH SERVICE
MEDICAL CARD
ISSUED BY THE
Shropshire Family Practitioner Committee
39 Abbey Foregate
SHREWSBURY, Shropshire, SY2 6BN

Please quote this number if you write to the Family Practitioner Committee
N.H.S. Number

DATE OF BIRTH

Mr., Mrs., Miss., ...
Address ....
....
.... Postcode ....

Please notify the Family Practitioner Committee of changes of name or address and return this card to them. Make sure you tell your doctor, too.

Dr: ....
....
.... Postcode ....

SA

Medical card issued by the National Health Service.

You will find the doctor, or in many cases his receptionist, only too pleased to help since English doctors who work for the National Health Service receive a substantial payment for each person on their register (whether or not they ever have to treat that person).

Other suitable excuses for requiring a new medical number include the following:

- You have been working abroad for several years and have lost track of what your number was or which doctor, if any, you were previously registered with.
- You have been working on a casual basis in different parts of the country for the past few years and never bothered to register with a doctor. Now, though, you intend to settle down.

No identification is required to obtain this document, but having a document which confirms your name and address will dispel any doubts on the part of the receptionist or doctor.

Choose large and busy city practices, rather than practices located in small towns. If possible, register with a group practice, which is a practice staffed by several doctors who share the patients. There are group practices in most major cities, and their addresses can be found in any local phone directory.

A little extra research can provide you with the names and addresses of doctors who have ceased to practice for one reason or another—retirement or death, for example. Such a name may then be used to support your claim for a new card. You can explain that you've been abroad for a few years and were surprised to learn upon your return to England that the doctor you used to go to is now deceased or retired, as the case may be. Be sure to act genuinely surprised, especially if any resistance to your explanation is felt.

Although it is not openly acknowledged, a doctor who is about to cease his practice should notify all his patients and refer them to other doctors. Anyone who does not reregister with another doctor—or the new doctor who has taken over the old practice and is now located at a different address—ends up in a sort of no-man's-land, neither on a list nor off it. Their old records are not transferred or brought up to date and, in many cases, are eventually destroyed or left to rot in some old filing cabinet. No one will go out of his way to cross-check your claims, providing you have chosen details that are far from simple to confirm or refute.

The addresses of surgeries that have closed down and the names of doctors who have retired or died can be found by checking through old directories and the obituary columns of newspapers or medical magazines. Such publications are available for inspection at all major libraries. When applying for a medical card, you will probably be asked whether you have ever been hospitalized for an operation; your answer must always be no. To answer otherwise entails the checking of hospital records in an attempt to assemble your medical details. If you bear the scars of an operation, explain that the surgery was performed abroad. Be sure to cite an obscure country as the place of your surgery—a country that is outside the realms of British interest.

BRITISH VISITOR'S PASSPORT

Because of the close links which exist between Britain and certain other countries, it is possible for a British citizen (the holder of a British passport) to travel to these countries on only a short-term, identity-card type of document known as a visitor's passport.

This passport is only valid for one year, after which time it must be renewed, and only the countries listed on the application form may be visited using this document. Apart from these conditions and bearing in mind the ease with which this document can be obtained, the visitor's passport is an extremely useful piece of paper to have. All the questions and answers concerning the issue of this document are included on the application form, an example of which is given on the following pages.

The person issuing the passport, who will no doubt be an overworked postal clerk, has the power to refuse a passport at his discretion. Reasons for refusal would have to be drastic; for example, if you claimed to be English-born, but were black and spoke with an American accent! If you resembled someone on a wanted poster or if your chosen name was one of 250,000 on the undesirables/wanted/suspected list, you may also be refused a visitor's passport.

It is best if you go to the office unprepared: ask for the application there and then have your picture taken on the spot, rather than bring a photo with you. (Note that the photo machines in England are close relatives of the one-armed-bandit, and the amount of money you feed into them bears little relation to what comes out!)

The information on the application concerning supportive documents needed in order to obtain a passport seems to be aimed at those who would change their names at the drop of a hat. However, it is said that they are included because they apply to women who may be getting married in the near future.

UNITED KINGDOM PASSPORT

The process for obtaining a British national's passport is quite simple—it's just the forms that make it look like hard work. The application, accompanying note sheets, and index cards are reproduced here in their entirety. Any questions you may have can be answered simply by studying the material. The fees noted are current at the time of this writing.

It will be readily seen that the only I.D. requirement is a birth certificate or adoption certificate and a couple of photos, one of which must be witnessed by a doctor, lawyer, teacher, or someone of similar standing. This witness, or referee, must be prepared to sign a declaration to the effect that he has known you for at least two years. (I suggest that, if possible, you find someone who will claim to have known you for a minimum of three or four years.) There are plenty of people with suitable qualifications who will sign such a declaration, either for financial reward or out of friendship. It is common practice for an individual to make friends with someone who falls into the required category, maintaining the friendship for a few months to a year. At that point, the would-be applicant explains to his friend that he has the opportunity to travel abroad, but does not know anyone who can sign the declaration. People who consider themselves friends will be only too pleased to "tell a white lie" and sign the declaration, exaggerating the amount of time they have known you. Remember to send them a postcard!

When I give—sorry, that should read when I *sell* —my advice to clients, I always recommend that they invest at least two years' time in their new

MISC 320

Stamp of issuing office	For official use only
	Passport number
	Documents produced by: Holder Spouse Children

Passport Office

Form VP

Application for a British Visitor's passport

Valid for one year only

for British citizens, British Dependent Territories citizens, or British Overseas citizens

of at least 8 years old who are resident in the UK, Isle of Man or Channel Islands

---

A Visitor's Passport can be used for holidays or unpaid business trips of up to 3 months to
Andorra
Austria
France (including Corsica)
Germany–Federal Republic (West Germany)
and by **air** to **West** Berlin

Gibraltar
Greece
Italy (including Sicily, Sardinia and Elba)
Liechtenstein
Malta
Monaco
Portugal (including Madeira and the Azores)
San Marino
Spain (including the Balearic and the Canary Islands)
Switzerland
Tunisia
Turkey

Belgium Luxembourg Netherlands	children under 16 years of age cannot go on their brother's or sister's passport
Denmark Finland Iceland Norway Sweden	Trips to these as a group must add up to less than 3 months in a 9 month period
Bermuda	
Canada	Your Visitor's Passport must be valid for one month after your last day in Canada.

Important
If you wish to travel to, or through, a country not listed above you must obtain a Standard British Passport

Application for a British visitor's passport.

ALL THOSE TO BE INCLUDED ON THE PASSPORT MUST BE **EITHER**:

a British citizen

OR a British Dependent Territories citizen

OR a British Overseas citizen

Visitor's Passports are **NOT**, however, definite evidence of National Status.

If you are not sure whether you have one of these citizenships, please ask the Passport Office for advice.

Belfast   Tel. 0232-232371
Passport Office
Grd. Floor Hampton House
47-53 High Street
Belfast BT1 2QS

Liverpool   Tel. 051 237 3010
Passport Office   Ext. 294
5th Floor India Buildings
Water Street
Liverpool L2 0QZ

Newport   Tel. 0633-56292
Passport Office   Ext. 226 or 236
Olympia House
Upper Dock Street
Newport Gwent NPT 1XA

Glasgow   Tel. 041-332 0271
Passport Office   Ext. 24 or 25
1st Floor
Empire House
131 West Nile Street
Glasgow G1 2RY

London   Tel. 01-213 3344
Passport Office   01-213 7272
Clive House   01-213 6161
70 Petty France   01-213 3434
London SW1H 9HD

Peterborough Tel. 0733-895555
Passport Office   Ext. 238
55 Westfield Road
Peterborough PE3 6TG

Dual Citizens
If you are a British citizen, British Dependent Territories citizen or British Overseas citizen and also a citizen of another country you cannot, when in that country, be protected by HM Government against the authorities of that country.

A Visitor's Passport
What documents are needed
One of the documents listed below is needed for **each** person to be included on the passport (photographic copies are not acceptable).
a A birth certificate or adoption certificate showing full names issued in the United Kingdom or abroad by a United Kingdom authority;
b A National Health Service Medical Card in your present name;
c A DHSS Retirement Pension Book or Pension Card BR464 in your present name;
d An uncancelled Standard British Passport or British Visitor's Passport in your present name (or husband's/wife's if included on it).

Photographs
2 recent, identical photographs size 50mm x 38mm (2" by 1½") of yourself (and 2 of your wife/husband if she/he is to be included on the passport). The photographs should be taken full face without a hat. Photographs are not required for an included child.

How much does it cost?
£7.50
£11.25 if wife/husband is to be included.

How and where do I get the passport?
By taking your completed application form, photographs, required documents (see above) and fee, **in person** (if your wife/husband is to be on the passport she/he must go with you. A child for whom a separate Visitor's Passport is required must also go with you) to:

in	England Wales Scotland	A Main Post Office ,, ,,	(Monday to Friday only)
in	Northern Ireland	Passport Office Hampton House 47-53 High Street Belfast BT1 2QS	(Tel 232371)
in	Jersey	Passport Office	St Helier (Tel 25377)
in	Guernsey	,,	St Peter Port (Tel 26911)
in	Isle of Man	,,	Douglas (Tel 26262)

Visitor's passports are not obtainable from mainland Passport Offices in Glasgow, Liverpool, London, Newport or Peterborough.

Wife/Husband included on the passport
can **only** use it when they are travelling with the holder

Children on the passport
Children can **only** be included on a parent's (or step-parent's/adoptive parent's), brother's or sister's passport and then **only** until they are 16 years old. When they are 16 or over, they must have their own passport. They cannot travel on their own using a passport in which they are only included.
Children under 8 cannot have their own Visitor's Passport.

Amendments to the passport
You cannot have the passport altered in any way after it has been issued e.g. you cannot have your wife/husband/child added to it.

Post-dated passports
You cannot have a Visitor's passport post-dated or issued in a future married name for your use immediately after your marriage.

Care of passports
Your passport is an important document. If you lose it you should inform the Police and the Passport Office, Glasgow. If you are abroad you should inform the nearest British Consulate or High Commission.

Passport holder (person whose name will appear on passport)

Please write clearly in ink using CAPITAL LETTERS

Mr. Mrs. Miss., Ms or title _____
Surname _____
Forename(s) or Christian name(s) _____
Maiden surname (if any) _____
Date of birth _____ Age _____
Town of birth _____ Country of birth _____
Present address in the United Kingdom _____
Postcode _____
Height in metres (see conversion table right) _____
Visible distinguishing marks (if any) _____

Particulars of wife/husband – if to be included on passport

Surname _____
Forename(s) or Christian name(s) _____
Maiden surname (if any) _____
Date of birth _____
Town of birth _____ Country of birth _____
Height in metres (see conversion table right) _____
Visible distinguishing marks (if any) _____

Children under 16 years of age – if to be included on passport

1 Surname _____
Forename(s) or Christian name(s) _____
Date of birth _____
Place of birth _____
Sex _____
Relationship to applicant (eg son, daughter) _____

2 Surname _____
Forename(s) or Christian name(s) _____
Date of birth _____
Place of birth _____
Sex _____
Relationship to applicant (eg son, daughter) _____

3 Surname _____
Forename(s) or Christian name(s) _____
Date of birth _____
Place of birth _____
Sex _____
Relationship to applicant (eg son, daughter) _____

4 Surname _____
Forename(s) or Christian name(s) _____
Date of birth _____
Place of birth _____
Sex _____
Relationship to applicant (eg son, daughter) _____

Parent's or guardian's consent for a person under 18 years old and for included children.

Not needed if the person is married or in HM Forces.
If the person is illegitimate their mother must give consent.
If a court order exists the person awarded custody of the child/children must sign.

I (full name) _____
of (address) _____
the (relationship to child/children eg father, mother) _____
being his/her/their legal guardian, apply for the issue of a Visitor's Passport for him/her/them.
I confirm that my rights over the child/children have not been altered by a court order
Signature _____

Photograph

Standard Passport holders

If you, or a child under 16 for whom you are applying, have a valid standard passport it must be given to the Post Office when you apply for a Visitor's Passport. The Post Office will keep the standard passport but you may apply to have it returned by writing to the Passport Office at which it was first issued and surrendering your Visitor's Passport.

If your wife/husband/child are to be included on your Visitor's Passport and they have a valid standard passport, it will **not** be kept by the Post Office.

The measurement of height

Height in passports is now shown in metric units. A conversion table follows

feet	inches	metres	feet	inches	metres
4	0	1.22	5	3	1.60
4	1	1.24	5	4	1.63
4	2	1.27	5	5	1.65
4	3	1.30	5	6	1.68
4	4	1.32	5	7	1.70
4	5	1.35	5	8	1.73
4	6	1.37	5	9	1.75
4	7	1.40	5	10	1.78
4	8	1.42	5	11	1.80
4	9	1.45	6	0	1.83
4	10	1.47	6	1	1.85
4	11	1.50	6	2	1.88
5	0	1.52	6	3	1.90
5	1	1.55	6	4	1.93
5	2	1.57	6	5	1.96

Please also fill in this index card ▶

Declaration–to be completed by all applicants

If the passport is for a child under 16 this must be filled in and signed by a parent

Do you/Does the child already have a passport?
please tick appropriate box

☐ YES ☐ NO

If your wife/husband is to be included on the passport does she/he already have a passport?
please tick appropriate box

☐ YES ☐ NO

If you have/the child has a passport already it should be given to the Post Office with this application
See Standard Passport holders (left)

If you cannot give the passport to the Post Office,

please state why   Date of
(eg lost or stolen)   loss/theft

Has the lost/stolen passport been reported to the police?
please tick appropriate box

☐ YES ☐ NO

If YES, please state
where and when

Number of lost/stolen
passport (if known)

Place of   Date of
issue   issue

If the passport is found by me or returned to me
I undertake to send it to the Passport Office, Glasgow or,
if I am abroad, to the nearest British Consulate or High Commission

I the applicant/I the wife/husband of the applicant declare that

I, and those to be included on the passport are British citizens, British Dependent Territories citizens or British Overseas citizens

that no other passport application is being made for me/us

that none of us have returned to the United Kingdom at HM Government expense and still owe the cost of the repatriation

that the information given is to the best of my knowledge correct and that I know that it is a criminal offence knowingly to make a false statement in this application

Signature of applicant   date

Signature of wife/husband   date
(if to be included on passport)

INDEX CARD

Please also fill in this index card

Surname of
passport holder

Forename(s) or
Christian name(s)

Place of birth

Date of birth

For official use only

Passport number   Stamp of issuing office

File number

identity in order to obtain genuine references from the local doctor or vicar.

The intervening time is also well spent, for in that time you can establish good credit records and reinforce your new identity. If you need a long-term or permanent identity, then this approach is definitely the way to go about it. Situations vary, of course, and you may require a passport quickly, in which case previously mentioned methods can be employed instead.

NEVER be tempted to create a fictitious name and address for the person acting as your referee. The British passport authorities *do* check to see if such a person exists. If you have forged a signature and given nonexistent address and occupation details, you will most certainly receive a visit from the Special Branch of Scotland Yard. At the very least, your movements will be monitored until such time as the investigating authorities determine whether or not you are dangerous. In any event, at the end of such time, you will receive a visit from the aforementioned authorities.

Under normal circumstances, however, the passport authorities will not check with a referee to verify his statement. I have seen a dozen or so passports which were obtained by citing existing persons as referees without their knowledge. It appears that the issuing authority cross-checks the electoral register to confirm the name, address, and profession of the supposed referee, and if all the information listed on the application checks out, the referee may not be contacted for statement verification.

The names and addresses of suitable "referees" can be found in the local electoral register, available for inspection at some libraries or a local registry office.

It is indeed possible to obtain a passport by bluffing on the referee section of the application form. Answer the questions on the form intelligently, and get a friend to complete and sign sections where referees or guarantors are required to make declarations.

The British passport authorities grudgingly admit that at peak application times, such as summer, they do not have the staff, cash, or time to cross-reference applications. They rely instead on the ability of officers to detect attempted frauds; if the obvious and easily checked statements do not check out, they delay issue until further inquiries can be conducted.

CHANGES TO A UNITED KINGDOM PASSPORT

Changes can be made to an existing passport by using the following form. The form is intended primarily for women who get married or other individuals who change their names legally. This is no quick way to a new identity, as the old name will be shown along with the new one. Similarly, if a new photograph is submitted because the holder has changed in appearance sufficiently to warrant it, the old photo will be retained when the new passport is issued.

UNION MEMBERSHIP CARD

Unlike American union cards, which often carry a statement to the effect that the holder is proficient in some skill or another, the English card is simply a visual record of dues paid. For the most part, the card shows only the name and trade or position of the holder and a year's worth of validation spaces which are filled in as the weekly or monthly dues are paid.

Union cards can be obtained upon request from the local branch offices of the various unions, the names and addresses of which can be found in any telephone directory. Many people who are unemployed join unions in England, as membership supposedly enhances employment opportunities; indeed, many firms will only employ persons who are in a union or prepared to join one with which that company has an exisiting agreement.

As can be seen from the sample application form, there is no evidential or supportive identification requirement, and the questions are very basic. No checking or cross-referencing is conducted. When applying, you will have to pay a percentage of the annual dues in advance, and the card will be issued on the spot. Unless you will be working for someone who will have union dues deducted from your wages on a weekly or monthly basis, you will have to send the dues to the local union office yourself. If you choose to pay in person, your card will be validated by the person who takes the dues from you (usually the guy behind the reception desk). However, if you send the money in, you can validate the card yourself. In fact, most people at work who pay

Please write in CAPITAL LETTERS and in ink   Passport Office

Your initials _____   Your surname _____

Date of travel _____

A Form
Application for United Kingdom Passport

Do use this form if you are in the United Kingdom and wish to apply for a UK passport.

Don't use this form if
you are under 16 – use Form B

your previous passport was for five years because you were under 16 – use Form D

you want a British Visitors Passport which is valid for one year and for short holidays in certain countries only. Application for those should be made at main Post Offices, or in Northern Ireland to the Passport Office, Hampton House, 47-53 High Street, Belfast BT1 2QS.

Read this section before you fill in the form
United Kingdom Passports are issued to British Citizens, British Dependent Territories Citizens, British Overseas Citizens, British Subjects and British Protected Persons.

Citizens of another Commonwealth country should apply to the Office of that country's High Commissioner.

Dual nationality: if you possess the nationality or citizenship of another country, you may lose this when you get a British Passport. Please check with the authorities of the other country before making your application.

How long does it take to get a passport? Please post or take your application to a Passport Office at least **four weeks** before you need your passport. During April to August applications take longer than at other times of the year.

If an emergency arises, or if you need a passport in less than four weeks, get in touch with your regional passport office (see **note 18**).

Notes *
There is a separate sheet of **Notes** to help you complete the form. Please refer to the **Notes** whenever the form tells you to.

NOW PLEASE TURN TO THE FORM ➡

Space below is for Passport Office use only
S/A _____
CBF _____

Space below is for Passport Office use only
Next action

Documents produced _____

Applicant's birth certificate _____

Wife/husband's birth certificate _____

Child's (or children's) birth certificate(s) _____

Marriage certificate _____

Nationality document _____

Other documents _____
_____

Photographs _____

Fee _____

Issue _____
(Status)

Observations _____

Include _____

Immigration status _____

Application for a United Kingdom passport.

Please write in CAPITAL LETTERS and in ink

1 TO BE FILLED IN BY ALL APPLICANTS

Tick correct box Mr ☐ Mrs ☐ Miss ☐ Ms ☐ or title _____

Your surname _____

Christian names or forenames _____

_____

Maiden surname (if applicable) _____

Tick correct box Married ☐ Single ☐ Widowed ☐ Divorced ☐ Separated ☐

Age last birthday _____ Country of birth _____

Present address _____

_____

_____ Postcode _____

Daytime telephone no. _____
(We may need to get in touch with you urgently)

Job/occupation _____

Town of birth _____

Date of birth _____

Country of residence _____

Height (in metres) _____ *See note 1 for a conversion chart

Visible distinguishing marks _____

Have you changed your name other than by marriage or adoption? Yes ☐ No ☐

What was your previous name? _____

Go to section 2a

2a Family passport
Do you wish to include your husband/wife on your passport? Yes ☐ No ☐

*Read note 2 then complete this section
Details of husband/wife to be included on your passport

His/her surname _____

Christian names or forenames _____

Maiden surname (if applicable) _____

Country of birth _____

Town and country of marriage _____

Date of marriage _____

Job/occupation _____

Town of birth _____

Date of birth _____

Country of residence _____

Height (in metres) _____ *See note 1 for a conversion chart

Visible distinguishing marks _____

_____

Daytime telephone no. _____
Go to section 2b

Please write in CAPITAL LETTERS and in ink

2b Is your husband/wife a British Subject, a British Citizen, or a British Dependent Territories Citizen by descent? Yes ☐ No ☐

*Read note 5, then give details in section 13

Has your wife been married before? Yes ☐ No ☐

*Read note 2, then give details in section 13
Go to section 3

3 Family passport
Do you wish to include one or more children on your passport? Yes ☐ No ☐

*Read note 3 then complete this section for each child

Christian names or forenames	Surname	Town and country of birth	Date of birth	Relationship to you (e.g. son or daughter)
1.				
2.				
3.				
4.				

For children born outside the U.K. and *all* children born *after* 31 December 1982

Father's full name _____

His town and country of birth _____

His date of birth _____

If father a citizen of the United Kingdom and Colonies, British citizen or British Dependent Territories citizen by naturalisation or registration.

No. of his document _____ Date of issue _____

Place of issue _____

Mother's full name _____

_____

Her town and country of birth _____

Her date of birth _____

If child born in foreign country and the birth was registered at a British Consulate

Name of British Consulate _____

Date of Registration _____

Has the name of the child or children changed? Yes ☐ No ☐

Give previous name _____

Go to section 4

4 Have you (or anyone included on this application) been naturalised or registered as a citizen of the United Kingdom and colonies, a British citizen, a British Dependent Territories Citizen, a British Overseas Citizen, or a British Subject? Yes ☐ No ☐

*Read note 4 and fill in details of citizenship documents

	You	Husband/wife	Children
Number			
Place of issue			
Date of issue			

Go to section 5

Please write in CAPITAL LETTERS and in ink

5 Were you born outside the United Kingdom? Yes ☐ No ☐

✱ **Read note 5** and complete this section
When did you become resident in the United Kingdom? _____

What is your father's full name? _____
_____

His town and country of birth _____

His date of birth _____

His nationality (and citizenship) when you were born _____

If your father became a British Subject or citizen of the United Kingdom and Colonies by naturalisation or registration, please give details of documents:

Number _____

Place of issue _____ Date of issue _____

Your mother's full name _____
_____

Her town and country of birth _____

Her date of birth _____

Was your birth registered at a British Consulate? Yes ☐ No ☐

Please give date of registration _____

Name of British Consulate _____

If your father was not born in the United Kingdom, please give the town, country and date of birth of your paternal grandfather (your father's father), or details of your paternal grandfather's claim to British nationality, in **section 13** (explained in **note 5**)

Go to section 6a

6a TO BE FILLED IN BY ALL APPLICANTS ✱ **Read note 6**

Have you had any sort of passport before or applied for any passport? Yes ☐ No ☐

Is your last passport attached? Yes ☐ No ☐

Previous passport number _____

Please complete **section 11**

Is your husband/wife to be included on your passport? Yes ☐ No ☐

Have they had any sort of passport before? Yes ☐ No ☐

Is their previous passport attached? Yes ☐ No ☐

Previous passport number _____

Please complete **section 11**

CAUTION
You are warned that the making of an untrue statement for the purpose of procuring a passport is a criminal offence. Passport Office procedures include a check on the authenticity of countersignatories. The application should not be countersigned until the form has been completed, signed and dated by the applicant.

Please write in CAPITAL LETTERS and in ink

6b Declaration To be signed by all applicants
And by husband/wife if they are to be included on your passport
I the undersigned, declare that

1 I have made no other application for a passport, other than that stated above.

2 (delete if not appropriate) If the passport mentioned in section 11 comes again into my possession, I will return it immediately to a British Passport issuing authority.

3 No one included on this application owes money to Her Majesty's Government for repatriation or similar relief.

4 I am a British Citizen or
British Dependent Territories Citizen or
British Overseas Citizen or
British Subject or
British Protected Person.
And I have not lost or renounced this status.

5 I (and any children shown in section 3) am/are today in the United Kingdom.

6 The information given in this application is correct to the best of my knowledge and belief.

Sign _____ Date _____

Your husband's/wife's signature (if he/she is to be included in your passport)
_____

Go to section 7

---

7 Declaration of parent— ✱ **Read note 7**

I (full name of parent) declare that my rights in respect of (insert names of child/children) _____
_____
have not been limited in any way by the order of any court having jurisdiction over him/her/them.

Signature _____ Date _____
Relationship to child _____ Daytime Tel. No. _____
Address _____
_____

Go to section 8

---

8 Countersignature THIS SECTION MUST BE COMPLETED BY THE COUNTERSIGNATORY

✱ **Read note 8**

1 Please read the CAUTION (left).

2 Endorse the back of the photograph by writing 'I certify that this is a true likeness of (insert name of applicant)' and add your signature.
For a family passport you should do the same for the husband/wife's photograph. Read what the applicant has put on this form, and

3 Fill in the following in capital letters and in ink
I (insert your name) _____
_____
certify that the applicant has been known personally to me for ☐ years, and that to the best of my knowledge and belief the facts stated on this form are correct. I am a Commonwealth Citizen.

Sign _____

Profession (and professional qualifications, if applicable)
_____

Name of firm, business address or official stamp (if applicable)
_____

Daytime telephone no. _____ Date _____

Go to section 9

Please write in CAPITAL LETTERS and in ink

9a Are you a married (or widowed or divorced) woman applying for your own passport? Yes ☐ No ☐

✱ **Read note 9** and complete this section
(Women who are getting married should **read note 2 and note 9**)

Town and country of marriage _____

Date of marriage _____
And these details of your husband (or late husband or former husband)
His full name _____

_____

His town and country of birth _____

His date of birth _____ His nationality _____

Date of divorce _____ Date of death (if applicable) _____
Have you been married more than once? Yes ☐ No ☐

Please give details of previous marriage(s) in **section 13**

9b Was your husband born outside the United Kingdom? Yes ☐ No ☐

Were you or your children born outside the United Kingdom? Yes ☐ No ☐

Full name of husband's father _____

_____

His town and country of birth _____

His date of birth _____
Did your husband become a British Subject or British Citizen (or citizen of the United Kingdom and Colonies) by naturalisation or registration? Yes ☐ No ☐

Please give details of documents
Number _____

Place of issue _____ Date of issue _____

Did your husband become a British Subject or British Citizen (or citizen of the United Kingdom and Colonies) because of his father's naturalisation or registration? Yes ☐ No ☐

Please give details of documents
Number _____

Place of issue _____ Date of issue _____
Go to section 10

10 TO BE COMPLETED BY ALL APPLICANTS
✱ **Read note 10**

Countries to be visited _____

Purpose of journey _____
Please give the names of two relatives or friends who can be contacted if you meet with an accident. This information will only be used in an emergency.
Name _____
Address _____

Telephone number _____ Relationship (if any) _____
Name _____
Address _____

Telephone number _____ Relationship (if any) _____

Please write in CAPITAL LETTERS and in ink

11 Details of previous passport which has been lost or is not available. ✱ **Read note 11**

Number _____ issued at _____

_____ in (year) _____

Your name at the time of issue _____

_____

How the passport was lost, or why it is not available _____

_____

_____

Date and place of loss _____

If loss was reported to the police, say where and when _____

_____

Now go back to sections 6a and 6b

12 Type of passport
If after reading **note 12** you need a passport of 94 pages, please tick the box ☐

13 Other information

_____
_____
_____
_____
_____
_____
_____
_____
_____
_____
_____
_____
_____

Checklist
when you have completed the form

Please check that you have all the enclosures:

Documents – see **note 13**

Fee – see **note 14**

Photographs – see **note 15**
(one certified on the back)

And remember to sign the form at **section 6b 'Declaration'** and, if appropriate, **section 7**

Enclosed the registered post fee – see **note 17**

IT IS IMPORTANT THAT ALL APPLICANTS NOW READ NOTES 13 TO 18.

Space below is for Passport Office use only

Printed in the UK for HMSO Dd 8422151 3/84 (28781) 1000M

Passport Office Form A

*Notes

United Kingdom Passport Application

Please keep these Notes until you receive your passport

Note 1
Conversion chart. Height in passports is shown in metres.

Feet	Inches	Metres	Feet	Inches	Metres	Feet	Inches	Metres
4	6	1.37	5	2	1.57	5	10	1.78
4	7	1.40	5	3	1.60	5	11	1.80
4	8	1.42	5	4	1.63	6	0	1.83
4	9	1.45	5	5	1.65	6	1	1.85
4	10	1.47	5	6	1.68	6	2	1.88
4	11	1.50	5	7	1.70	6	3	1.90
5	0	1.52	5	8	1.73	6	4	1.93
5	1	1.55	5	9	1.75	6	5	1.96

Note 2
A husband/wife may not be included on a family passport if he/she already holds a separate valid United Kingdom Passport. Details of a husband/wife may be included in a passport at the time of issue but cannot be added at a later date. A family passport is meant to enable families to travel together. It can be used by the husband/wife in whose name it is issued when travelling alone but not by the included husband/wife independently. **(Please read note 6.)**

If your wife has been married more than once details of any previous marriage(s) – i.e. former huband's full names, his nationality and place and date of birth, date of marriage, date of divorce (if applicable), date of former husband's death (if applicable) – should be given in section 13.

If the husband/wife to be included in the family passport is a British Citizen by descent or a British Subject, details should be given in section 13. **(Please read note 5.)**

If your marriage took place on or after 1st January 1949 and your wife was not a British Subject at the time of the marriage, her details cannot be included in a family passport unless she has now become a British Subject by registration. Nor can they be included if she is a citizen of another Commonwealth country and is not at the same time a British Citizen, a British Dependent Territories Citizen or a British Overseas Citizen.

If you are getting married and want to travel abroad on a family passport immediately after your wedding you should get Forms PD 1 and PD2. **(Please read note 9.)**

Note 3
Section 3 should be filled in if children under 16 years of age who are related to you are to be included in the passport. These children cannot use the passport to travel without you. Only children who are British Citizens, British Dependent Territories Citizens, British Overseas Citizens, British Subjects or British Protected Persons, and do not themselves hold valid United Kingdom Passports, may normally be included. Only children who are actually in the United Kingdom at the time of application may be included. Where the children are in another country, application for United Kingdom Passport facilities for them should be made to the nearest British Passport issuing authority in that country.

If any of the children to be included in the passport, and either of their parents, were born outside the United Kingdom, you should give in section 13, the town, country and date of birth, or claim to British nationality, of all four of their grandparents.

Children aged 16 and over need separate passports.

Note 4
Section 4 should be filled in if you became a British Subject or citizen of the United Kingdom and Colonies by naturalisation or registration before 1 January 1983, or if you have become a British Citizen, British Dependent Territories Citizen, British Overseas Citizen or British Subject by naturalisation or registration on or after that date. If your husband/wife and/or children to be included in the passport were naturalised or registered please fill in the second and third columns as appropriate.

Note 5
Section 5 should be filled in if you were born outside England, Scotland, Wales and Northern Ireland. But it need not be filled in if you became a British Subject, citizen of the United Kingdom and Colonies, British Citizen, British Dependent Territories Citizen, or British Overseas Citizen by naturalisation or by registration at the Home Office, London.

If you were born in a foreign country, in the Republic of Ireland, or in a part of the Commonwealth other than a place which is still a dependent territory you may be able to claim British Citizenship, British Dependent Territories Citizenship or British Overseas Citizenship through your father if he was a British Subject and citizen of the United Kingdom and Colonies. But if your father also was born outside England, Scotland, Wales and Northern Ireland, or a place which is still a dependent territory, you should give in section 13 the town, country and date of birth, or claim to British nationality of your paternal grandfather (your father's father) in case you have a claim to British nationality by descent from him.

Note 6
If you hold a British Passport, a British Visitor's Passport, a Commonwealth Passport, a foreign passport or other travel document of any description you should tick YES.

If you have not held a passport or travel document of any kind you should tick NO.

If you were included in your husband's/wife's British Passport, you should enclose it with this application so that your particulars may be deleted from it.

If you were born abroad, and you have not previously held a passport of your own, please give details in section 13 of the passport on which you travelled to this country.

If you are unable to write, you should impress a left thumb print as signature. The impression should be witnessed by the person who completes section 8 of the form.

Note 7
Section 7 should be filled in and signed by a parent if the applicant is under 18 years of age, except where the applicant is married (in which case the marriage certificate should be produced) or is enlisted in HM Forces. If a child is to be included on the passport of a relative other than a parent, this section should be filled in by a parent of the child. If the parent is not available to sign the form, he/she must write a letter of consent. The letter should be sent in with the application. If the applicant or child to be included in the passport is illegitimate, consent should be given by the mother.

Note 8
When you have completed the form, section 8 should be completed and signed by a Member of Parliament, Justice of the Peace, Minister of Religion, Lawyer, Bank Officer, Established Civil Servant, School Teacher, Police Officer, Doctor or a person of similar standing who has known you personally for at least two years and who is either a British citizen or a British subject or a citizen of a Commonwealth country. A member of your family should not countersign. **(See also note 15 'Photographs'.)** Passport Office procedures include a check on the authenticity of countersignatories. In certain cases you may be asked to produce further documentary evidence of identity.

Note 9

Part A should be filled in unless you are returning a standard blue British Passport (not a British Visitor's Passport) which was issued in your present name and neither you nor any children included at section 3 were born outside England, Scotland, Wales and Northern Ireland.

If you have been married more than once, details of any previous marriage(s) – i.e. former husband's full names, his nationality, his town, country and date of birth, date of marriage, date of divorce (if applicable), date of former husband's death (if applicable) – should be given in section 13.

Part B should also be filled in if your husband was born outside England, Scotland, Wales and Northern Ireland, and if in addition you or any children to be included in your passport were born outside those countries. If your husband and also his father were born outside England, Scotland, Wales and Northern Ireland (or a place which is still a dependent territory), the town, country and date of birth or claim to British nationality of your husband's paternal grandfather (his father's father) should be given in section 13.

If you want to amend your existing passport to show your new married name, you should get Form G (fee £3.00). But if you are getting married and want to travel abroad on a separate passport immediately after your wedding you should get Forms PD1 and PD2 for the issue of a post-dated passport in your future married name OR for the amendment of your existing passport to show your future married name with post-dated effect. **(See also note 2.)**

Note 10

Your passport will be made valid for all countries in the world. But it is to your advantage to state the countries you wish to visit and the purpose of your journey. This will enable us to advise you about passport problems which may arise in certain countries.

Note 11

Please give as much information as you can. A new passport can be issued only after extensive enquiries.

Note 12

A standard United Kingdom Passport of 30 pages is adequate for most travellers and is valid for 10 years.

However, a passport of 94 pages is available for people who travel a lot and quickly fill the visa pages of a standard passport. This passport is also valid for a maximum of 10 years.

When you apply for a new passport, you must give up any previous passport. A new passport may not be post-dated to the date of expiry of a previous passport.

Note 13
DOCUMENTS TO BE PRODUCED
Photographic copies of birth, marriage or naturalisation certificates or registration documents are not acceptable for passport purposes.

These tables show which documents you should produce with your application. Please read all the sections that apply to you and make sure that you submit the right documents. Documents are not normally needed if you are surrendering an unrestricted blue British Passport and all details are the same. Documents ARE required if a British Visitor's Passport only is being surrendered.

Since birth in the United Kingdom after 31 December 1982 will not automatically confer British Citizenship, in some cases you may be asked for additional information and documentation to establish national status under the provisions of the British Nationality Act 1981 which came into effect on 1 January 1983.

TABLE 1 – BIRTH BEFORE 1 JANUARY 1983

a If you were born in England, Scotland, Wales, Northern Ireland, the Channel Islands, the Isle of Man or a place which is still a Dependent Territory.

All applicants
Birth (or adoption) certificate. If in doubt, read **note i**, '**Birth certificate**'

Women who are or have been married and married men under 18
Marriage certificate or Divorce documents showing details of the marriage. If in doubt, read **note ii** '**Marriage certificate/Divorce documents**'.

---

b If you were born outside England, Scotland, Wales, Northern Ireland, the Channel Islands, the Isle of Man, and a place which is still a dependent territory, of a father who was a British Subject and citizen of the United Kingdom and Colonies and who, became, or but for his death would have become, a British Citizen, a British Dependent Territories Citizen or a British Overseas Citizen under the provisions of the British Nationality Act 1981, OR

if you were born before 1 January 1949, in a Protectorate, Protected State or Trust Territory of a British father.

All applicants
Full Consular birth certificate showing parents' names, and evidence of father's citizenship of the United Kingdom and Colonies if this is not shown on the Consular birth certificate (see **note i**) OR

Full Local or High Commission or Forces birth certificate showing parents' names; parents' marriage certificate, and father's birth certificate, naturalisation or registration document, or other evidence of father's national status (see **note i**).

Women who are or have been married and married men under 18
Marriage certificate
or Divorce documents showing details of the marriage (see **note ii**)

---

c If you are a British Subject, a British Citizen, a British Dependent Territories Citizen, a British Overseas Citizen or citizen of the United Kingdom and Colonies by naturalisation or registration.

All applicants
Documents of naturalisation or registration.

Women who are or have been married and married men under 18
Marriage certificate
or Divorce documents showing details of the marriage (see **note ii**).

---

d If you were a British Subject before 1st January 1949, through your own or your father's birth or naturalisation in British India or in the Republic of Ireland and have remained a British Subject (without citizenship).

All applicants
Documentary evidence of your birth or naturalisation in British India or in the Republic of Ireland or documentary evidence of legitimate descent from a father born or naturalised in those territories (see **note i**).

Women who are or have been married
Marriage certificate or Divorce documents showing details of the marriage (see **note ii**).

---

e If you were born outside England, Scotland, Wales, Northern Ireland, the Channel Islands, the Isle of Man, and a place which is still a dependent territory, and you acquired citizenship of the United Kingdom and Colonies by adoption in the United Kingdom between 1st January 1950 and 31 December 1982, inclusive.

If adopted after 31 December 1982 see Table 4.

If adopted abroad consult Passport Office.

All applicants
Full adoption certificate showing names of adoptive parent(s) and documentary evidence that the adoptive parent was a British Subject and citizen of the United Kingdom and Colonies (see **note i**).

Women who are or have been married and married men under 18
Marriage certificate or Divorce documents showing details of the marriage (see **note ii**).

---

f If you acquired British nationality by marriage before 1st January 1949

All applicants
Birth certificate (or previous standard blue British passport). Marriage certificate or Divorce documents showing details of the marriage. Documents establishing your husband's (or former husband's) nationality as at **a, b, c** or **d** above (see **note ii**).

TABLE 2—BIRTH BEFORE 1 JANUARY 1983
If you are applying for a family passport
Your own and your husband's/wife's documents as in **a, b, c, d, e** or **f**.
Marriage certificate or previous family passport (see **note ii**).

TABLE 3
If children under 16, and born before 1 January 1983, are to be included in your passport
Their documents as in **a, b, c** or **e**.

TABLE 4
If children under 16 and either born or adopted after 31 December 1982 are to be included in your passport.
If child born in England, Scotland, Wales, Northern Ireland, the Channel Islands or the Isle of Man
Child's birth (or adoption) certificate

If parents are not British Citizens, their passports as evidence of residence in the United Kingdom.

If child adopted, full adoption certificate showing names of adoptive parent(s) AND documentary evidence that the adoptive parent is a British Citizen.

If child born outside England, Scotland, Wales, Northern Ireland, the Channel Islands or the Isle of Man
Child's full Local, Consular, High Commission or Forces birth certificate showing parents' names, plus:

if mother born in the United Kingdom, her birth certificate;

if father born in the United Kingdom, his birth certificate and marriage certificate;

if neither parent born in the United Kingdom, evidence that the mother is a British Citizen otherwise than by descent e.g. registration document, naturalisation certificate, or similar evidence that the father is a British Citizen, otherwise than by descent, and his marriage certificate.

If child is a British Citizen by registration
Child's registration document.

TABLE 5
If name has been changed otherwise than by marriage or adoption
Documents as in Table 1 AND
Documentary evidence (e.g. deed poll, statutory declaration) that your name has been changed for all purposes. Similar evidence (if appropriate) in respect of your husband/wife or children if they are to be included in your passport.

Note i. Birth certificate
If you were born in England or Wales you can obtain a birth certificate by calling or writing to the local Register Office of the district in which you were born; any Registrar of Births and Deaths will tell you the appropriate address. Alternatively you can apply to the General Register Office, St. Catherine's House, 10 Kingsway, London WC2B 6JP. Telephone 01-242 0262 Ext. 2446/7/9. You should apply to St. Catherine's House if:

you are unsure of your place of birth; OR

you are a British Subject born abroad; OR

you have a birth or adoption certificate which does not show your place or country of birth or your full name.

If you were adopted in England or Wales since 1927 you can obtain a certificate from the Adopted Children Register by calling at St. Catherine's House or by writing to the General Register Office, Titchfield, Fareham, Hants PO15 5RU. Telephone Titchfield (0329) 42511 Extension 288.

If you were born in Scotland you can obtain a birth certificate from the local Registrar for the district in which your birth was registered. Any Registrar of Births, Deaths and Marriages in Scotland will give you the appropriate address and also the fee for a Short or Full Certificate. If you write it will be helpful if you can give your full name, date and place of birth and the full names of your parents, including mother's maiden name.

You can also purchase a birth certificate by calling at, or writing to the General Register Office for Scotland, New Register House, Princes Street, Edinburgh EH1 3YT (Telephone 031 556 3952). It will normally take at least 7 days and may take up to 21 days to obtain a certificate.

Please note that if you were adopted in Scotland, Short or Full Certificates from the Adopted Children Register can only be obtained from General Register Office, New Register House.

For births which occurred in Northern Ireland or the Republic of Ireland apply respectively to the Registrar-General, Oxford House, 49/55 Chichester Street, Belfast BT1 4HL or the Registrar-General, 8/11 Lombard Street East, Dublin 2.

Note ii. Marriage certificate/Divorce documents
A divorce decree is normally acceptable instead of a marriage certificate. A married (or widowed, or divorced) woman applying for a separate passport is not normally required to produce her marriage certificate if she is surrendering her previous United Kingdom Passport (not a British Visitor's Passport) in the same married name, or if she can produce a previous United Kingdom family passport (not a British Visitor's Passport) in the same name. The marriage certificate must be produced, however, if application is being made for a family passport, unless a previous United Kingdom family passport (not a British Visitor's Passport) in the same name is being returned.

Note 14

Fee
The fee for a United Kingdom Passport of 30 pages
1) without particulars of wife/husband £15
2) including the particulars of wife/husband £22.50

The fee for a United Kingdom Passport of 94 pages (see note 12)
1) without particulars of wife/husband £30
2) including the particulars of wife/husband £45
You should send the money with your application.

If application is made by post please make payment by cheque or postal order payable to the Passport Office and crossed 'A/C Payee'; in the case of a cheque please also write on the back the full name and address of the person in whose name the passport is to be issued. Cheques will be accepted from personal callers only if supported by a cheque card. Should a cheque be returned to the Passport Office by the bank for any reason, the drawer may be required to pay any additional charges incurred. Issue of a passport may be delayed until the matter is resolved.

If paying by Giro transfer add the words 'Passport Fee' after the amount in words (e.g. Fifteen pounds – Passport Fee) and leave the credit account number blank. You must, however, send the transfer document with your passport application.

Note 15

Photographs
Please send two identical copies of a recent photograph of yourself (and also two of your husband/wife if you are applying for a family passport). Photographs are not required of children to be included in your passport.

The photographs should be taken full face without a hat. The size should not be more than 63 mm by 50 mm (2½ inches by 2 inches) or less than 50 mm by 38 mm (2 inches by 1½ inches). They should be printed on normal thin photographic paper and be unmounted.

The person who countersigns your application (see **note 8**) should also write on the back of ONE photograph the words 'I certify that this is a true likeness of Mr, Mrs, Miss, Ms or title . . .' and add his/her signature.

If you are applying for a family passport one of your husband's/wife's photographs should be similarly endorsed and signed by the same countersignatory.

Note 16
How to send your application

Please send the application by post, or take it to a Passport Office at least four weeks before you need the passport.

When posting the application enclose your passport and any necessary documents. Write your name and address on the back of the envelope, and keep a note of the **exact** date of posting.

Taking your application to a Passport Office may mean queuing and does not guarantee priority treatment.

If you live in England or Wales, the Passport Office for your area is shown below, each area office is represented by initial letters, thus: Liverpool **Li**; London **Lo**; Newport, Gwent **N**; Peterborough **P**.

Avon **N**	Kent (less London boroughs) **P**
Bedfordshire **P**	Lancashire **Li**
Berkshire **N**	Leicestershire **P**
Buckinghamshire **P**	Lincolnshire **P**
Cambridgeshire **P**	Merseyside **Li**
Cheshire **Li**	Middlesex **Lo**
Cleveland **Li**	Mid Glamorgan **N**
Clwyd **Li**	Norfolk **P**
Cornwall **N**	Northamptonshire **P**
Cumbria **Li**	Northumberland **Li**
Derbyshire **Li**	North Yorkshire **Li**
Devon **N**	Nottinghamshire **P**
Dorset **N**	Oxfordshire **N**
Durham **Li**	Powys **N**
Dyfed **N**	Shropshire **N**
East Sussex **N**	Somerset **N**
Essex (less London boroughs) **P**	South Yorkshire **Li**
Gloucestershire **N**	Staffordshire **Li**
Greater London **Lo**	South Glamorgan **N**
Greater Manchester **Li**	Suffolk **P**
Gwent **N**	Surrey (less London boroughs) **N**
Gwynedd **Li**	Tyne and Wear **Li**
Hampshire **N**	Warwickshire **P**
Hereford and Worcester **N**	West Glamorgan **N**
Hertfordshire (less London boroughs) **P**	West Midlands **P**
	West Sussex **N**
Humberside **Li**	West Yorkshire **Li**
Isle of Wight **N**	Wiltshire **N**

If you live in Scotland the Passport Office is in Glasgow.

If you live in Northern Ireland the Passport Office is in Belfast.

Full addresses are given below.

Addresses

Belfast
Passport Office, Hampton House,
47-53 High Street, Belfast BT1 2QS
Telephone Belfast 232371

Glasgow
Passport Office, 1st Floor, Empire House
131 West Nile Street, Glasgow G1 2RY
Telephone 041-332 0271

Liverpool
Passport Office, 5th Floor, India Buildings
Water Street, Liverpool L2 0QZ
Telephone 051-237 3010

London
Passport Office, Clive House
70 Petty France, London SW1H 9HD
Telephone 01-213 3344, 01-213 6161, 01-213 7272, 01-213 3434.

Newport
Passport Office, Olympia House
Upper Dock Street, Newport, Gwent NPT 1XA
Telephone Newport 56292

Peterborough
Passport Office, 55 Westfield Road, Peterborough PE3 6TG
Telephone Peterborough 895555

Normal hours of business
Mondays to Fridays, 9 am to 4.30 pm

Cases of emergency arising outside normal hours of business
A duty officer is available in London as follows to deal with cases of emergency only (e.g. death or serious illness) which cannot be submitted during normal business hours.
Mondays to Fridays, 4.30 pm to 6. pm
Saturdays, 10 am to 12 noon
Documentary evidence of the emergency should be produced.

Note 17
Return of passports
Passports and documents are sent out from Passport Offices by first class post. If you want yours to be returned by registered post please send £1.25 to cover the cost.

Note 18
Enquiries after application has been sent
If possible, you should send your application at least **four weeks** before the passport is needed. Please do not make enquiries if you do not receive it within this period. However, if an emergency arises, you should get in touch with your area Passport Office and give the following information:

your full name;

your place and date of birth;

how the application was lodged, for example

by post stating the exact date of posting OR

personally at a Passport Office, stating the date of your receipt and its reference number in full.

Applications sent during April-August take longer to process than those sent at other times of the year.

British Nationality Act 1981

From 1 January 1983 no endorsement about immigration status is necessary on passports issued to British Citizens as they will automatically be exempt from United Kingdom immigration control and have the right to take up employment or to establish themselves in business or other self-employed activity in another member state of the European Community.

The relevant Member States of the EC are BELGIUM, DENMARK, FRANCE, FEDERAL REPUBLIC OF GERMANY, GREECE, ITALY, LUXEMBOURG and NETHERLANDS. But the free movement of labour provisions will not be applicable to Greece until 1 January 1988.

The EC provisions relating to the free movement of labour and the right of establishment do not apply to Channel Islanders and Manxmen unless they can show that they have a close connection with the United Kingdom itself through birth, descent, adoption, naturalisation, registration or residence.

Passports issued to British Dependent Territories Citizens, British Overseas Citizens, British Subjects or British Protected Persons will be endorsed to show their immigration status. In some cases it may be necessary to ask for additional information in order to determine that status.

Printed in the UK for HMSO Dd 8422151 3/84 (28781) 1000M

INDEX CARD		Surname (IN BLOCK CAPITALS)	
	Passport No.	Christian names (or Forenames) in full (IN BLOCK CAPITALS)	
	Space below is for Passport Office use only	Date of birth	Place and country of birth
		Particulars of spouse (if to be included in the same Passport) Christian Names (or Forenames) in full (IN BLOCK CAPITALS)	
		Date of birth	Place and country of birth
		Space below is for Passport Office use only No. Issued.	

PLEASE COMPLETE IN BLOCK CAPITALS THE INDEX CARD ABOVE AND THE TWO LABELS BELOW WHICH WILL BE USED, WHERE NECESSARY, TO ACKOWLEDGE RECEIPT OF YOUR APPLICATION AND TO DESPATCH YOUR PASSPORT TO YOU IF YOU ARE NOT COLLECTING IT IN PERSON.

Printed in the UK for HMSO Dd 8303322 4/83 99196·1

(Name) ....

(Address) ....

....

....

(Name) ....

(Address) ....

....

....

Please fill in passport holder's name

Please write in CAPITAL LETTERS and in ink

Please write holder's present name unless name is to be changed on marriage in which case put future married name

Initials   Surname

Date of travel

File number

G Form
Application for changes to United Kingdom passport

if you are in the United Kingdom and wish to:
- ★ amend the name on your passport
- ★ add a recent photograph
- ★ amend your personal details on page 2 of passport

if you hold a British Visitor's Passport

a If your name has been changed by marriage you should provide the marriage certificate. Photographic copies are **not** acceptable for passport purposes.

b If your name has been changed other than by marriage documentary evidence such as a deed poll, or statutory declaration is required.

Please post or take your application to a Passport Office at least four weeks before you need your passport.

During April to August applications take longer.

Please don't make enquiries if you don't receive the passport within the four week period.

However, if an emergency arises, you should get in touch with your area Passport Office and give the following information:

a your full name as shown on the passport and, if this has been changed, your new name;

b your place and date of birth;

c how the application was made, for example

★ If by post then state the date of posting OR if personally at a Passport Office state the date of your receipt and its reference number in full.

NOW PLEASE TURN TO THE FORM

Space below is for Passport Office use only

S/A

CBF

Space below is for Passport Office use only

Next action

Documents produced

Passport

Marriage certificate

Photographs

Other documents

Fee

1 Amend

2

3

4

5 Amend national status to

Application for changes to a United Kingdom passport.

If the passport holder is under 16 the person who fills in this form must be an adult. If this adult is not a parent of the child, a letter from a parent (giving consent) must be sent with the application. If the passport holder is illegitimate, consent should be given by the mother.

If the passport holder is **aged 16 or 17** and neither married nor an enlisted member of Her Majesty's Forces, a parent should complete and sign Section 4 or write a separate letter of consent and send it with the application. If the applicant is illegitimate, consent should be given by the mother. A married passport holder aged 16 or 17 should produce the marriage certificate.

The Passport Office will change your name by adding the words:
'NOW MR/MRS/MISS/MS/ OR TITLE' (followed by new name) beneath your original name on the front and on page 1 of your passport.

Only one change of name can be made.

If you are intending to travel abroad straight after the wedding please fill in this form:

★ for a change to your passport showing your future married name

Get leaflet PD1 and forms PD2 & 3 for this purpose.

Height in passports is now given in metres (eg if your height is 5 feet 6 inches then write in 1.68 metres).

feet	inches	metres	feet	inches	metres
2'	6" =	0.76m	4'	6" =	1.37m
2	7 =	0.79	4	7 =	1.40
2	8 =	0.81	4	8 =	1.42
2	9 =	0.84	4	9 =	1.45
2	10 =	0.86	4	10 =	1.47
2	11 =	0.89	4	11 =	1.50
3	0 =	0.91	5	0 =	1.52
3	1 =	0.94	5	1 =	1.55
3	2 =	0.97	5	2 =	1.57
3	3 =	0.99	5	3 =	1.60
3	4 =	1.02	5	4 =	1.63
3	5 =	1.04	5	5 =	1.65
3	6 =	1.07	5	6 =	1.68
3	7 =	1.09	5	7 =	1.70
3	8 =	1.12	5	8 =	1.73
3	9 =	1.14	5	9 =	1.75
3	10 =	1.17	5	10 =	1.78
3	11 =	1.19	5	11 =	1.80
4	0 =	1.22	6	0 =	1.83
4	1 =	1.24	6	1 =	1.85
4	2 =	1.27	6	2 =	1.88
4	3 =	1.30	6	3 =	1.90
4	4 =	1.32	6	4 =	1.93
4	5 =	1.35	6	5 =	1.96

Please write in CAPITAL LETTERS and in ink

Passport number _____ Date of issue _____
Where issued _____

Tick correct box   Mr ☐   Mrs ☐   Miss ☐   Ms ☐   or title _____

Surname (shown on passport) _____

Christian names or forenames _____

Maiden surname (if applicable) _____

Date of birth _____

Town and country of birth _____

Present address _____
postcode _____

Daytime telephone number
(We may need to get in touch with you urgently) _____

Is a change required to the name in which the passport was issued?   Yes ☐   No ☐

New name of holder

Tick correct box   Mr ☐   Mrs ☐   Miss ☐   Ms ☐   or title _____
Surname _____

Christian names or forenames _____

Are you a woman whose name has been or will be changed by marriage?   Yes ☐   No ☐

Present or future husband's full names _____

Present or future husband's town and country of birth _____

His date of birth _____   Date of your marriage _____

Town and country of marriage _____

Is a change required to the personal details on the passport?   Yes ☐   No ☐

☐ Change profession to	☐ Change profession to
☐ Change country of residence to	☐ Change country of residence to
☐ Change height to: metres	☐ Change height to: metres
☐ Change visible distinguishing marks to	☐ Change visible distinguishing marks to
☐ Add new photograph	☐ Add new photograph

Please write in CAPITAL LETTERS and in ink

Warning
Applicants are warned that the making of an untrue statement for the purpose of obtaining a passport is a criminal offence

↓

Are you a parent signing for a child aged 16 or 17?   Yes ☐   No ☐

Your full name _____

Your address _____

postcode _____

Your relationship to child (tick a box)   Father ☐   Mother ☐   Daytime telephone No. _____

Signature of parent _____   Date _____

Sign

↓

I declare that:
1 the particulars given in this application are correct;
2 the passport holder does not owe money to Her Majesty's Government for repatriation or similar relief and that
3 he or she is today in the United Kingdom

Sign   Date _____

tick correct box   Father ☐   Mother ☐   Adult (not father or mother) ☐

↓

6 Are you a woman applying for the passport to be amended to your future married name?   Yes ☐   No ☐

If yes, give **future** married name signature

Sign   Date _____

↓

Checklist for when you have completed the form
tick boxes to show that you have:

inserted the holder's name and date of travel on page 1 ☐
enclosed any necessary documents and photographs ☐
enclosed passport ☐
enclosed all the fees ☐
signed the form ☐

The photograph in a passport must remain, but if it no longer looks like you or has been damaged or lost then a new one can be added. For this purpose send two identical copies of a recent photograph. They should be taken full face without a hat. The size should not be more than 63mm by 50mm (2½ inches by 2 inches) or less than 50mm by 38mm (2 inches by 1½ inches). They should be printed on normal thin photographic paper and be unmounted.

The back of one photograph should be endorsed with the words 'I CERTIFY THAT THIS IS A TRUE LIKENESS OF Mr/Mrs/Miss/Ms or title. . .' by a British Citizen or a British Subject or a Commonwealth Citizen who knows you personally and who is:

a Member of Parliament, Justice of the Peace, Minister of Religion, Doctor, Lawyer, Bank Officer, Established Civil Servant, School Teacher, Police Officer, or a person of similar standing. They should add their signature, profession and date.

A member of the applicant's own family should **not** endorse the photographs.

The duplicate photograph retained by us when the passport was issued cannot be used in place of a damaged or missing photograph.

Over 16

a If you want the holder's name amended the fee is £3.00 (section 2).

b If you want the holder's personal details on page 2 amended AND/OR if you want a recent photograph of the holder added the fee is £3.00 (section 3).

Under 16

If you were under 16 when you got your passport you only have to pay for a change of name.

No fee

If the passport is in your name and you want changes made to your wife's or husband's personal details only.

If applying by post make your payment by cheque or postal order payable to the 'PASSPORT OFFICE' and crossed 'A/C PAYEE'.

If paying by cheque write your full name and address on the back.

Cheques will be accepted from personal callers only if supported by a cheque card.

Should a cheque be returned to the Passport Office by the bank for any reason, the drawer may be required to pay any additional charges incurred.

Cash should not be sent by post.

If paying by GIRO transfer add the words 'PASSPORT FEE' after the amount eg 'THREE POUNDS – PASSPORT FEE' and leave the credit account number blank. Remember to send the transfer document with your application.

Return of passports

Passports and document are sent out from Passport Offices by First Class post. If you want yours to be returned by registered post please send £1.25 to cover the cost.

Please send the application by post, or take it to a Passport Office at least four weeks before you need the passport.

When posting the application enclose your passport and any necessary documents. Write your name and address on the back of the envelope, and keep a note of the **exact** date of posting.

Taking your application to a Passport Office may mean queuing and does not guarantee priority treatment.

If you live in England or Wales, the Passport Office for your area is shown below. Each area office is represented by initial letters, thus: Liverpool **Li**; London **Lo**; Newport, Gwent **N**; Peterborough **P**.

Avon **N**	Kent (less London boroughs) **P**
Bedfordshire **P**	Lancashire **Li**
Berkshire **N**	Leicestershire **P**
Buckinghamshire **P**	Lincolnshire **P**
Cambridgeshire **P**	Merseyside **Li**
Cheshire **Li**	Middlesex **Lo**
Cleveland **Li**	Mid Glamorgan **N**
Clwyd **Li**	Norfolk **P**
Cornwall **N**	Northamptonshire **P**
Cumbria **Li**	Northumberland **Li**
Derbyshire **Li**	North Yorkshire **Li**
Devon **N**	Nottinghamshire **P**
Dorset **N**	Oxfordshire **N**
Durham **Li**	Powys **N**
Dyfed **N**	Shropshire **N**
East Sussex **N**	Somerset **N**
Essex (less London boroughs) **P**	South Yorkshire **Li**
	Staffordshire **Li**
Gloucestershire **N**	South Glamorgan **N**
Greater London **Lo**	Suffolk **P**
Greater Manchester **Li**	Surrey (less London boroughs) **N**
Gwent **N**	Tyne and Wear **Li**
Gwynedd **Li**	Warwickshire **P**
Hampshire **N**	West Glamorgan **N**
Hereford and Worcester **N**	West Midlands **P**
Hertfordshire (less London boroughs) **P**	West Sussex **N**
	West Yorkshire **Li**
Humberside **Li**	Wiltshire **N**
Isle of Wight **N**	

If you live in Scotland the Passport Office is in Glasgow.

If you live in Northern Ireland, the Passport Office is in Belfast.

MISC 318

Belfast
Passport Office
Hampton House, 47-53 High Street, Belfast BT1 2QS
Telephone Belfast 232371

Glasgow
Passport Office, 1st Floor, Empire House
131 West Nile Street, Glasgow G1 2RY
Telephone 041-332 0271

Liverpool
Passport Office, 5th Floor, India Buildings
Water Street, Liverpool L2 0QZ
Telephone 051-237 3010.

London
Passport Office, Clive House
70 Petty France, London SW1H 9HD
Telephone 01-213 3344, 01-213 6161, 01-213 7272, 01-213 3434.

Newport
Passport Office, Olympia House
Upper Dock Street, Newport, Gwent NPT 1XA
Telephone Newport 56292

Peterborough
Passport Office, 55 Westfield Road, Peterborough PE3 6TG
Telephone Peterborough 895555

Mondays to Fridays, 9.00am to 4.30pm

Cases of emergency arising outside normal hours of business
A duty officer is available in London as follows to deal with cases of emergency only (e.g. death or serious illness) which cannot be submitted during normal business hours.
Mondays to Fridays, 4.30pm to 6pm
Saturdays, 10am to 12 noon

Documentary evidence of the emergency should be produced.

Passport Office,
Printed in the UK for HMSO
Dd 8422178 4/84 AWO Ltd.

Sign here!

Amount paid at time of Admission	

☐

PLEASE COMPLETE IN BLOCK LETTERS
I desire to become a member of the T. & G.W.U. in Scale

Name...

Address..

....

Date of Birth..

Trade or industry engaged in..

Work performed..

Name and address of employer..

Are you, or have you been, a member of this or any other Trade Union?................

Give the name of the Trade Union or Branch of this Union of which you are or were formerly, a member...

If you are a membe   any other Trade Union, and are not in benefit state amount of your arrears...

If you were formerly a member of this or another Trade Union, state reasons for leaving...

In the event of being admitted a member of the Union are you prepared to conform to all its Rules and Regulations, and such alterations as may be made in them from time to time in accordance with the constitution of the Union?.................

Signature ....

Date of Application..

SCALE 2 DECLARATION.

I (name in full)...
do herewith make application to be admitted as a member of the Incapacity Fund of the Transport and General Workers' Union.

　I agree to undergo a medical examination at any future date if called upon to do so, and to abide by the decision of the Medical Officer, and if it be proved that the following answers are false and that my health was not of satisfactory condition at the date of this application, I agree to release the Transport and General Workers' Union from any liabilities and claims which I may have upon them, and to refund the amount of any benefit which may have been paid to me, and that my membership of the Incapacity Fund shall be cancelled.

Questions	Answers
1. Are you in sound health and of good constitution?	
2. Are you at present suffering from any ailment or accident?	
3. Have you suffered from any chronic disease or accident during the last three years?	

Signature ....

MEMBERSHIP NO..................

BRANCH..................

Typical union application.

union dues validate their own cards. The validation actually takes the form of scribbling an illegible signature in the appropriate week or month box. No official stamp is used. In practice, few people working for others bother to fill in the weekly record of dues paid as they know the union headquarters has a record of payments. For identification purposes (although the cards are not intended as identification in the true sense of the word), be sure your card is always paid up to date.

Such cards are becoming more widely accepted as identification, due perhaps in part to the large number of unemployed persons, many of whom would otherwise have no other proof of identity to regularly carry on their person. In fact, the post office now accepts the union card as evidence of identity when cashing Girobank checks—the method of payment for persons receiving state benefits. Union cards can also be used as identification when opening a post office savings account or withdrawing money from such an account.

You will find that the effect a union card produces in England varies considerably according to where you are and what you are trying to achieve. In many industrial areas where the unions have a firm hold, a paid-up union card can open a few doors and turn borderline projects to your favor.

TRAVEL PASS

An excellent addition to anyone's I.D. collection, a travel pass is easy to acquire. There are different types of passes in England, and each one is issued by a different local authority which entitles the holder to differing amounts of travel. The amount you save over regular fares is considerable, since the passes are valid for rail and bus travel. The passes, though, can only be used within the boundaries of the issuing authority. (A pass issued by the West Midlands authority, for example, may only be used on the West Midland transport buses and trains.)

Applicants have to provide two photographs, both of which are taken on the premises of the pass-issuing authority. The staff selects the "best likeness," and the other photo is returned or destroyed.

No evidential identification is requested, and few of the offices keep records. In the words of one office staff member, "if you lose the card, tough luck." It is apparent that you can be whoever you choose when applying for such passes, and the card itself can be used to substantiate your new identity. Plenty of people have used such cards as identification when opening bank accounts or obtaining credit. Some even have used it as I.D. when arrested by the police in order to get themselves out on bail. So if you find yourself near an office selling the passes, be sure to get one, or three!

2. AUSTRALIA

Rumor had it, when I began researching this book, that Australia was one of the easiest places in the world in which to obtain new identification. As this evaluation had been made public, I fully expected the regulations to have been tightened considerably—especially regarding birth certificates. This is not the case, however, and despite government pressure on departments to cross-reference birth and death certificates, the practice has not been adopted as of this writing. In the words of one very helpful official, "Given a budget increase of $10,000 and an increase in staff of fifty percent, we might be able to handle it—just."

BIRTH CERTIFICATE

The birth-certificate forms, examples of which are given here, do ask the applicant to state why he or she desires the certificate, which may be a certified copy or an "extract." The best reason for you to give is that your relative has asked you to obtain a copy of the certificate so that he or she can apply for a passport. Or, you can say that *you* are the person to whom the certificate relates and you have lost the original. Other excuses are given elsewhere in this book, and there are plenty that will occur to you when the need arises.

Minor variations in format and fees exist in the different states, and as with other subjects, it would not be practical to list them all herein. Fee variations will only run to a couple of dollars at most, and the format of the application will vary according to the attitude of the department head. It is a simple matter to make general inquiries and ascertain which state is the least restrictive.

The parental information required to secure the certificate can be gleaned from church records, library archival material which details deaths, or by the time-tested technique of touring the graveyards. Specific methods given throughout this book can, of course, also be used.

"CLIPBOARD SPECIAL"

Another technique that has been used in Australia in the past, but is by no means limited to that area, is known in some circles as the "cilpboard special." Requirements for this method are a clipboard and a hard neck.

In any large city, on any given day, there can be seen, hovering around street corners, a variety of persons armed with clipboards and a smile whose intention it is to solicit information from passersby on every subject under the sun. (The reliability of public transportation, the price of butter, and the likelihood of a nuclear holocaust occurring before the interviewer has time to write down the answers are but three examples!) For your purposes, the questions to ask concern the efficiency of local funeral directors, the attitude of credit companies toward relatives of recently deceased persons who owed the company money, or the long-term effects of bereavement on a surviving spouse. There are plenty of similar subjects that will enable you, the interviewer, to extract enough information from interviewees to support an application for a birth certificate.

It is important that the questions are well thought out and questions which relate to personal details—place of birth, mother's maiden name, for example—are camouflaged among more general questions. It is obvious that only a small percentage of persons interviewed will have been unfortunate enough to have lost a son or daughter while the child was young. You must therefore tailor the questions so that this fact is established very early on in the interview; if the person has not suffered such a loss, you can then cut the interview short. A percentage of the people you approach will not even wish to answer your questions, and if this is the case, smile politely and target someone else. Be professional about the project, and it will be a success. Do not rush

Births Deaths & Marriages Registration Division
59 King William Street
ADELAIDE 5000

BIRTH

G.P.O. Box 1351
ADELAIDE 5001
This Receipt MUST be produced when collecting documents

| | Received amount printed by cash register |

(Tick appropriate boxes)

Please supply ☐ Extract or ☐ Certificate

to be ☐ Posted ☐ Collected ☐ Priority Service

COMPLETE IN BLOCK LETTERS

Surname ....
(If Female; Insert Maiden Name)
Given Names ....
Date of Birth .... Sex ....
Place of Birth ....
Father's Name (in full) ....
Mother's Maiden Name (in full) ....

Reg. No.

Book........ Page........

You are advised that a certified copy includes **any former married name(s) of the mother.** A copy MAY be supplied omitting this information. Please indicate if you wish this information to be omitted.

☐ place tick in box

Relationship of Applicant and
reason for application ....

Signature ....
Address ....
....

NOTE:—If Birth occurred within 6 months of application, state at which hospital

....

Australian birth certificate application.

Births Deaths & Marriages Registration Division
59 King William Street
ADELAIDE 5000

DEATH

G.P.O. Box 1351
ADELAIDE 5001
This Receipt MUST be produced when collecting documents

Received amount printed by cash register

(Tick appropriate boxes)

Please supply ☐ Extract or ☐ Certificate

to be ☐ Posted ☐ Collected ☐ Priority Service

Reg. No.

Book......... Page.........

COMPLETE IN <u>BLOCK</u> LETTERS

Surname ....

Given Names ....

Date of Death— Day .... Month .... Year ....

Place of Death ....

Age of Death ....

Usual Residence ....

Relationship of Applicant and
reason for application ....

Signature ....

Address ....

NOTE:—If Death occurred within last 6 months, state name of funeral director

The "note" box in the bottom right-hand corner of the death-certificate application form implies that information pertaining to the death may still be on file at the funeral director's office six months after the death. A visit to various undertakers, with a view to confirming the demise of a "friend" or "relative," could be very helpful to you in obtaining death and/or birth record information!

up to someone and shout, "Hey, have any of your kids died?" since to do so will not generate the type of response you desire. Rather, try something like, "Excuse me, I wonder if you would care to answer a few questions? I'm afraid they are rather personal, but are part of a research project that may prevent a lot of suffering in the future on the part of parents who suffer the loss of a child in infancy or early childhood." This statement explains immediately what sort of questions you are likely to ask, and if the subject has not had such an experience, he will normally say so right away. If you find an individual who has experienced such a loss, he often may be only too pleased to discuss the subject.

Colleagues of mine who put this technique to the test recently gave the following report. One Saturday afternoon in a major Australian city, a team of three interviewers stopped to interview a total of four hundred people. Of that total, seventy would not take part in the project at all; 320 explained that they were unmarried, had no children, or had not experienced the death of their child; and nine knew of others who had lost children during birth or in infancy. One subject had lost his seven-year-old son in a car accident which had also killed his father. She was quite willing to discuss the matter and provide (unknowingly) enough information to enable another team member to apply for a birth certificate in the name of the deceased child.

The odds of this technique's success may not appear to be high, and luck and the interviewer's skill may play a large part in acquiring the information you need. However, the technique has been used successfully, so it is worthy of inclusion here. Should you try such a method, be sure you have a credible excuse for soliciting the information. Perhaps you can say you are a freelance journalist, for example, who is working on a project which you hope to sell at a later date, or a novelist researching material for a book. These covers are useful should a police officer inquire as to your project.

ASSUMING THE IDENTITY OF A DECEASED ADULT

Remember that if you decide to be the "ghost" of someone who died later on in life, the clipboard technique can achieve even better results since the percentage of persons interviewed who have lost a spouse or adult child will be far higher than those who have lost a young child. Vary the questions accordingly, and learn how to "fish"—that is, learn how to ask questions without actually asking them. (If you have no idea of what I mean by this, then this is not the approach you should undertake.)

As mentioned in previous chapters, assuming the identity of someone who died as an adult is a touch more risky than becoming the ghost of an infant or youngster. The reason for this is that one has to assume that an adult would have generated more information about himself which may well be on record, and a percentage of that information may be negative. However, if your final area of operations is to be in an area located some distance from the former neighborhood of the deceased, the chances that you will meet someone who knew him are negligible.

I would not advise you to completely rule out using the identity of a deceased adult, however. If you apply some thought and effort in selecting a suitable candidate, run your own credit checks to ascertain the person's character, and use the identity some considerable distance from the deceased's hometown or place of work, you will not encounter too many problems.

It would be stupid, of course, to adopt the identity of someone who was widely known or who had an unusual name. Assuming you find a suitable "Mr. Average," the following steps can be taken to establish whether or not the identity is worth having. First, apply for some low-level credit using your new name. If your application is successful, apply for a major credit card in order to create solid credit information. Use an accommodation address on all applications. If there is no problem with the credit applications you have submitted, you can then apply for a driver's license. If you are not asked to provide details of previous addresses or other information that may indicate your identity is being questioned, your next step is to apply for a passport.

Note that unless you can verify that the individual whose identity you are to adopt has not been issued a passport, there is considerable risk involved in making an application yourself. One very basic check used by passport-issuing authorities is to cross-reference the surname of new applicants against those of people who have had passports issued to them. If the surname matches one of a person who does have a passport (which is very common, of course) a first-name check is applied. Should the first names match (less common but more frequent than one might think), the date of birth and other details are cross-referenced. If *these* particulars match, the results are obvious.

So, how can you check whether or not the deceased person had been issued a passport? Well, the easiest way is to contact friends or relatives of the deceased and obtain the information under the pretense of statistical or genealogical research. If the initial information is to be obtained using the "clipboard special" technique, it is a simple matter to include a few questions concerning the travels (or lack of) of the deceased.

DRIVER'S LICENSE

Any person learning to drive in Australia is required to obtain a learner's permit, which allows him to drive under conditions stated in the permit; for example, he must have "L" plates on his car and be accompanied by a qualified driver. This permit is issued only *after* the applicant has passed the rule test. (Full details and example questions are given in a book entitled *The Road Traffic Code,* which is recommended reading if you intend to apply for the Australian driving test.) Proof of age may be required before the permit is issued, so be prepared!

Once a driver has passed the practical driving test, the Learner's Permit can be converted to a Probational License, and the "L" plates can be changed for "P" plates. This license is valid for a period of one year. Assuming the driver does not commit any vehicular offenses during that time, the license will be reclassified as qualified (nonprobationary).

A medical certificate will be required if you wear glasses or suffer from any minor illness. (Serious illness will, of course, prevent you from obtaining a license.) States will have minor variations regarding application and fee conditions, but a few inquiries will soon reveal which area is best suited to your requirements.

Inquiries and documentation requests pertaining to driving licenses should be made to a local Motor Registration Office. Names and addresses will be found in any local telephone directory. Application forms may also be completed at local country police stations. The rules test may be conducted in a language other than English, but a fee is payable for translation!

Persons taking up residence in Australia who hold a valid license issued by another country or a license that has expired during the previous three years may be exempted from the practical part of the driving test. You must, however, pass the rules test.

STUDENT I.D. CARD

A student I.D. card, easily obtained in Australia and most other countries, has become a more widely used and accepted form of identification in the last few years.

Obviously, a card that carries a photograph of the holder will prove more effective in many situations than one that has no photo, though either type of card can be extremely useful. Cards issued by the various colleges or universities vary, as do the requirements for obtaining them. In the majority of cases, it is simply a matter of registering with a college for a course and completing the various forms they issue. In some cases, you will be required to provide a photograph. An I.D. card will then be sent to you in the mail or given to you personally when you start the course. Some student I.D. cards are used to ensure that undesirables cannot easily get onto a college campus or into a university building, while others enable the holder who is presumably taking a course (full- or part-time) to enter other colleges or universities and make use of their libraries for study purposes.

Some travel organizations—and there are several of these in Australia—will grant reduced rates to students, as will certain sporting or recreational authorities. Where the application for an I.D. card is separate from the normal registration procedure, the information an applicant is required to submit is very basic. Apart from checking on any educational qualifications claimed by the applicant, colleges very rarely, if ever, check out the background of a potential student. This is especially true if the student is from out of state and wishes to only take a part-time course. Of several colleges contacted, some stated that a birth certificate was required as evidential identification, while others indicated a driving license would do. Some colleges, however, have no formal I.D. requirements at all; the individual completes an application form, and, where applicable, pays the fees, in whole or in part, in advance.

The student I.D. card shown below is from the University of Adelaide. In order to obtain a card at this university, an applicant must satisfy the issuing body that he is registered with the university (usually achieved by obtaining the signatures of course tutors). Where references are required regarding character or previous educational qualifications, you can expect that they will be checked. Of course, if you have been a resident of Australia for only a short time, but have undertaken some type of work while there, a letter of reference from your employer will be sufficient. Since Australian colleges and universities have many older students, individuals who have decided to improve their education later in life, your age will not arouse suspicion when you inquire about registration.

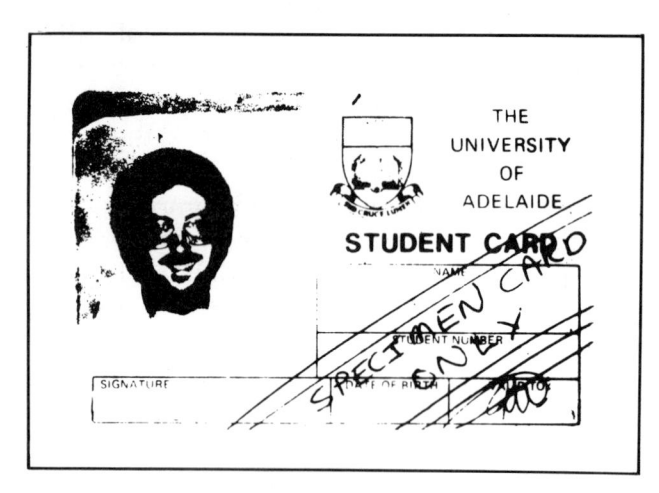

This Adelaide University student I.D. card is typical of those issued by Australian colleges and universities. Possession of such a card entitles the holder to cheap travel and other benefits.

MEDICAL CARD AND NUMBER

There is no national health service card as such in Australia. In order to obtain the Australian equivalent, one must register with either the government sponsored Medicare system or a recognized private company. Payment for the Medicare system is added to a person's income tax, but provisions exist for noncitizens to enroll. The application is simple, and no evidential identification is required from the applicant. However, authorities often check whether an applicant is registered to vote, as required by law.

An example of a Medicare application form is shown below, giving enrollment details. The section which explains that an individual should take care to ensure that he or she does not appear on more than one enrollment form is interesting, as it implies a less-than-effective screening process. For residents, the fees are one percent of taxable earnings, which generates a Medicare payment equal to the medical treatment fees incurred if the doctor bills Medicare direct. If he bills the individual, the system is slightly different.

Whether you apply for membership as a citizen and resident or as a visitor will depend on your ultimate aims. In either case, the Medicare membership card or a private equivalent serves as excellent identification. Since it pertains to the holder's health and welfare, few people would carry invalid or forged cards.

PASSPORT

The Australian passport application form, shown below, clearly explains all the whos, whens, and hows of obtaining an Australian passport. It also lists the addresses of the various passport offices. Note that applicants are required to present the application in person and attend an interview!

Although the application form states that referees or guarantors may be contacted by the passport office for statement verification, research indicates that this rarely, if ever, occurs. It would seem that the officer attending the applicant's personal interview relies on his experience to establish whether or not the applicant is "genuine." Obviously, the more out of the ordinary the application is, the more suspicious the officer will be; he is then quite likely to request additional information. If you provide the required documents and can act the part without becoming overly nervous or flustered, you will have no problems securing a passport.

SOCIAL SECURITY NUMBER

The Social Security card as issued and used in the United States does not really exist in Australia. Rather than to try to explain how to ask for an Australian Social Security number, using excuses similar to those outlined elsewhere in this book, I have included details pertaining to unemployment benefit claims. As the application forms shown on the following pages illustrate, the Australian system is geared to processing applications from persons of varied nationalities. The burden of proof regarding identity and eligibility rests with the applicant, who is required to submit evidence of identity even before the personal interview stage is reached.

TRAVEL PASS

The Austrailpass, only available outside Australia, allows unlimited first-class rail travel in Austra-

ENROLMENT APPLICATION

FOR PERSONS RESIDING IN AUSTRALIA

RETURN TO ANY MEDICARE OFFICE OR POST TO GPO BOX 9822 IN YOUR STATE CAPITAL CITY

TO BE COMPLETED BY PERSONS ENROLLING OR WISHING TO AMEND PRESENT ENROLMENT DETAILS

PLEASE PRINT ALL DETAILS

① **APPLICANT** (person who will receive the Medicare Card)

SURNAME _____ INITIALS _____

MR / MRS / MISS / MS

③ **PHONE CONTACT NUMBERS**

HOME _____

BUSINESS _____

② **RESIDENTIAL ADDRESS** [MUST BE COMPLETED]

_____

Postcode _____

④ **MAILING ADDRESS** [COMPLETE ONLY IF DIFFERENT FROM RESIDENTIAL ADDRESS]

_____

State or Territory _____ Postcode _____

⑤ **LIST ALL PERSONS TO BE SHOWN ON THE MEDICARE CARD**

SURNAME	FIRST GIVEN NAME & SECOND INITIAL	SEX M/F	DATE OF BIRTH (Day / Mth / Year)	Is the person already enrolled? Yes/No	If enrolled, show details from present Medicare card — Medicare No. / Surname (if changed)	Complete this section if a person listed is not a permanent Australian resident — Arrival Date / Departure Date / Name of Home Country
	e.g. ROBIN G					

If insufficient space please attach additional list

I declare that to the best of my knowledge & belief all information provided is true & correct.

Signature of Applicant _____ Date _____

Reason for visit to Australia _____

(EN1) 9/84

Enrollment application for a medical card and number.

ADVICE ON ENROLLING, OR AMENDING PRESENT ENROLMENT DETAILS

This application form is only for persons residing in Australia. A separate application form is available for Australian residents temporarily residing outside Australia.

If you are eligible for Medicare benefits the following information will help you decide the type of enrolment you need. Please read it carefully before completing the form. Further information is provided in the Medicare brochure, or may be obtained from your Medicare office.

ELIGIBILITY

All persons who reside permanently in Australia and persons visiting Australia for more than 6 months are eligible for Medicare benefits in Australia.

For services outside Australia, only Australian residents temporarily overseas are eligible for Medicare medical benefits.

Members of diplomatic missions and consular posts in Australia and their families are not eligible for Medicare benefits.

GENERAL

- You have the choice of enrolling either as an individual or as part of a family.
  IF SEEKING INDIVIDUAL ENROLMENT A SEPARATE APPLICATION FORM MUST BE COMPLETED FOR EACH PERSON. (Additional enrolment applications are available at Medicare offices.)

- The purpose of enrolment is to help you (and your family) to claim your Medicare medical benefits and to confirm your entitlement to free accommodation and treatment by staff doctors in a public hospital.

- Your card will be sent to you after this application form has been processed. You should have the card with you when seeking medical or hospital services or when making claims at a Medicare office.

THE APPLICANT

- The applicant (normally the person to whom cheques and correspondence will be sent) can apply for an individual card for herself/himself or for a dependant; or for a family card which can include dependent children and other relatives who live with the applicant.

- An application form may be filled out by another unrelated person, if the applicant is not able to complete the form (e.g. by the matron of a nursing home on behalf of a patient, or by a foster parent). All enrolment details, including the applicant's name, must relate to the person on whose behalf the application is being made.

- If the applicant is not able to sign the application, *the agent signing on their behalf must state this fact and the nature of their association with the applicant.*

- The person signing the application is responsible for the information on the enrolment form being correct. Care should be taken that an individual DOES NOT appear on more than one enrolment form.

FAMILY ENROLMENT

- Related people living in the same house may, for convenience, choose to be on a family card.

- In a family enrolment, the applicant's name and personal details must be listed as the first entry in Section 5, followed by details of other members of the family.

- PLEASE ENSURE that you list ALL persons in Section 5 who are to be shown on the Medicare card issued as a result of this application. This is important whether it is an enrolment requiring the issue of a new card number, or an amendment to the details shown on an existing Medicare card.

- Each Medicare card will show details of up to six people. Where there are more than six people in a family enrolment, an extra card will be issued.

- If it is more convenient for parents to have dual family cards, a second card will be supplied on request after March 1984.

INDIVIDUAL ENROLMENT

Anyone can apply for an individual card. The following persons may find it more convenient to have their own Medicare card:

- Single, working members of a family still living at home.

- Aged parents or grandparents living in the family home.

- A member of the family who is frequently away from home e.g. service personnel, truck drivers, itinerant workers.

- Children living away from home, e.g. in a boarding school, hostel, flat etc.

- Single people including widows and widowers and those living in a retirement village or nursing home.

A non related person who lives with the family, e.g. boarder, housekeeper, should always apply for an individual card.

Australia Post

APPOINTMENT

Post Office_____   Time_____

Telephone No._____   Date_____

<u>APPLICATION FOR PASSPORT</u>

When lodging your Passport Application, you are required to attend in person. However, an unmarried minor is not required to accompany a person lodging an application on the minor's behalf.

It is important that <u>each</u> change of name from that shown on the birth certificate is supported by documentary evidence. For example, each change of name through marriage must be supported by a marriage certificate.

To avoid any inconvenience in waiting for your application to be processed, please call at your local official Post Office or telephone the Postmaster at the above number and arrange an appointment for an interview.

Please read carefully the Information Notes contained in the Application Form. When lodging your application, you will be required to present the following documents:

<u>All applicants</u>
- Full Birth Certificate of Applicant showing details of both parents.
- Two photographs of correct size – please read photograph requirements on Application Form.
- Other means of identification, e.g., Driver's Licence, Credit Cards, etc.
- Fee $30.00.

<u>As applicable</u>
- Full Birth Certificate of children to be included on your Passport.
- Marriage Certificate – if name changed through marriage (extract acceptable).
- Citizenship Certificate – if Australian Citizenship acquired by grant of citizenship.
- Previous Australian Passport.
- Foreign Passport.
- Court Order/s relating to guardianship/custody/access of children under the age of 18 years.
- Full Death Certificate/s of Parent/s of children under the age of 18 years.

- Statutory Declaration is required when –
    - a name is changed by Deed Poll and the Deed Poll is not available;
    - a name is changed by reputation (except WA);
    - no place of birth is shown on a birth certificate of a person born in Australia; and
    - a person/s whose consent is required under Section 9 of the Application Form cannot be readily contacted (contact Postmaster for details).

N.B. Photocopies of the above documents are <u>NOT</u> acceptable. Extracts are also <u>NOT</u> acceptable (except Marriage Certificate extracts).

<u>Postmaster</u>

Application form for an Australian passport.

MS914 – DEC. 84

Department of Foreign Affairs

AUSTRALIAN PASSPORT APPLICATION

WARNING ▶ Under Section 10 of the Passports Act 1938, any person who makes a false or misleading statement whether orally or in writing to obtain an Australian passport or renewal or endorsement thereof or to support an application by another person is liable to a penalty of two years imprisonment. Passports obtained by this means can be confiscated on demand by an authorised officer.

IMPORTANT ▶ Before completing this application read the Information Notes below and refer to the instructions over the page as you complete each section. Failure to complete all relevant sections on the form or to provide all documentation required will result in delay in issuing a passport.

Under Regulation 5 (2) of the Passports Act an authorised officer may require an applicant to furnish such further evidence in relation to any application under these Regulations as the officer deems necessary.

INFORMATION NOTES

WHAT IS AN AUSTRALIAN PASSPORT: An Australian passport is a travel document issued by the Australian Government normally to Australian citizens only, to facilitate travel overseas.

WHO MAY APPLY: Normally an application may be submitted by an Australian citizen only. Children under 18 may apply for their own passport or may be included on the passport of another person with the proper consent.

WHAT IS THE VALIDITY OF A PASSPORT: Normal validity is five years and cannot be extended. If children are included the validity cannot exceed the date on which the eldest child turns 18.

WHAT SECTIONS TO COMPLETE IN THE FORM:

All applicants:
Sections 1, 2, 4, 5, 6, 7, 8, 10 and 11

and as applicable
- If under 18 — Section 9
- If children included — Sections 3 and 9

WHAT TO SUBMIT WITH THE FORM:

All applicants:
- Full birth certificate showing details of both parents
- Evidence of Australian citizenship where not acquired by birth
- Two identical photographs (see information note below)
- Passport fee of $30

and as applicable
- Any current Australian or foreign Passport (see instructions 5 and 6).
- Evidence of change of name (see instruction 1.)
- Documents for child/ren (see instructions 3 and 9).
- Other evidence as the interviewing/authorised officer deems necessary, eg. credit cards, driver's licence, etc.

DOCUMENTS: All documents submitted **must be originals**. Certified copies issued by the State/Territory Registrars of Births, Deaths and Marriages are considered to be originals. Applicants submitting foreign language documents must include translations from the Department of Immigration and Ethnic Affairs.

EVIDENCE OF AUSTRALIAN CITIZENSHIP: Citizenship must be demonstrated by submitting one of the following documents:—
- Ordinary Australian passport issued after 26 January 1949 which describes your national status as an Australian citizen.
- Australian birth certificate showing your place of birth in Australia: certified copies showing both parents must be submitted.
- Australian registration of birth overseas*
- Certificate of Citizenship*
- Declaratory Certificate of Citizenship*
- Evidentiary Certificate of Citizenship*

*These documents are issued by the Department of Immigration and Ethnic Affairs.

PHOTOGRAPHS: The photographs submitted must meet the following requirements:
- Two identical photographs no more than 6 months old.
- If children are included in the application the photographs **must show the applicant and children together.** (Horizontal format group photographs are acceptable)
- Size 45 x 35 mm as per diagram.
- Full front view of head and shoulders without head covering or sun/tinted glasses against a blank background.
- Dark backgrounds, automatic machine, fading or heat sensitive photographs are not acceptable. Photographs of doubtful clarity or likeness will be rejected.
- Reverse of one photograph to be certified and signed by the person providing the "Certification Regarding Applicant" as follows "**I certify this to be a true photograph of** (insert name or names in full)"

45 x 35 mm

Do not pin, staple or glue photograph to the application form

FEE: $30 AUSTRALIAN: Cheques, money orders, postal orders are acceptable and should be made payable to the Collector of Public Moneys. Cash should not be included with postal applications. Overseas applicants should pay the local currency equivalent after confirmation of the amount by the nearest Australian Mission.

WHERE TO APPLY: You must present your application and attend for a personal interview at an Official Australia Post Office, an Australian Passport Office, or if overseas an Australian Embassy, Consulate or Commission.

Addresses of Australian Passport Offices are:-

A.C.T. 22 West Row, CANBERRA CITY 2601.
Phone (062) 61 3801

N.S.W. Commonwealth Government Centre, Cnr Hunter and Phillip Sts, SYDNEY 2000. Phone (02) 221 1255

Mercantile Mutual Building, 456 Hunter St, NEWCASTLE 2300. Phone (049) 26 3655

VIC. Commonwealth Government Centre, Cnr Latrobe and Spring Sts, MELBOURNE 3000. Phone (03) 662 1722

S.A. Sun Alliance Building, 45 Grenfell St, ADELAIDE 5000. Phone (08) 212 2466

QLD Commonwealth Government Centre, 295 Ann St, BRISBANE 4000. Phone (07) 225 0122

W.A. St. Martin's Tower, 44 St George's Terrace, PERTH 6000. Phone (09) 325 4944

TAS. 4th Floor, T&G Building, Cnr. Collins and Murray Sts, HOBART 7000. Phone (002) 20 4050

N.T. Arkaba House, Esplanade, DARWIN 5790.
Phone (089) 81 4566

HOURS OF BUSINESS: 9.30 am-4 pm.

INSTRUCTIONS

SECTION

1. NAME

Enter your present surname and given names in full.

Change of Name: When applying in a name other than your name at birth **submit evidence of the change or changes of name** so that your current name can be traced back to your name at birth:

- If change of name by marriage/s — submit Marriage Certificate/s
- If change of name by registered deed poll — submit Deed Poll.
- If change of name by reputation — submit Statutory Declaration giving full details of change, usage in and acceptance of name by community **Note:** Change of name by reputation is not permitted in Western Australia.

Women about to marry: If you are within 6 weeks of being married and require a passport in your proposed married name complete two applications, one in your present name and one in your proposed name. You should also **submit** the following additional documentation:

- A letter from a person who will officiate at the ceremony certifying your intent to marry, showing the date and place of marriage, and full name of future spouse.
- A statement giving proposed travel details (date of departure and countries to be visited).

NOTE: If the marriage does not take place the passport must be returned to the place of issue for cancellation. Should you require a passport in your current name you must submit a new application and fee.

2. PERSONAL PARTICULARS

Place of Birth: If born outside Australia country of birth is optional and will appear in the passport only if shown on the form.

3. UNMARRIED CHILDREN UNDER 18 YEARS OF AGE WHOSE NAMES YOU WISH INCLUDED IN YOUR PASSPORT

Children may be included in one passport only. **Submit a full birth certificate (showing details of both parents)** for each child and evidence of Australian citizenship if acquired other than by birth.

NOTE: Validity of the passport will not extend beyond the date the eldest child turns 18 years.
If born outside Australia the inclusion of country of birth is optional.
Children may not use the passport for travel unless accompanied by the holder of the passport.

4. ADDRESSES

Complete **both** the residential address and the name and address label in full. Passports to be forwarded by post are sent certified mail.

5. PREVIOUS AUSTRALIAN PASSPORT:

If your current passport has been lost, stolen or destroyed, you must complete a form "Report of Loss/Destruction of an Australian Passport" (PC2) and **submit** it with this application or separately to the nearest Passport Office or Overseas Mission. The loss/theft should also be reported to the local police and where possible a copy of the report should be **submitted** with the PC2.

6. FOREIGN CITIZENSHIP:

If you hold citizenship of another country **submit** details of how and when this citizenship was acquired and details of any current foreign passport that you are holding.

7. SPECIMEN SIGNATURES:

Both specimen labels should be signed using your normal signature. If the applicant is a child who can legibly sign his/her name then the child should sign the labels, otherwise "unable to sign" should be written on each label.

8. PERSON TO NOTIFY IN CASE OF EMERGENCY

This information is required to enable the nominated person to be notified should you become distressed in any manner whilst overseas. The person nominated should, where possible, be resident in Australia and should not be accompanying you overseas.

9. CONSENT OF PARENTS/GUARDIANS

If the applicant is under 18 **and married** the consent of parents/legal guardians **is not required** however the applicant **must submit** the Marriage Certificate.

This section must be completed by each person who has legal custody, guardianship or access to the child/ren named in Sections 1 or 3.

If you have sole custody/guardianship without another party having legal access or guardianship evidence must be **submitted.** (Divorce Decree Absolute, Custody Order or Death Certificate of other parent.)

If you are unable to obtain the consent but consider the physical or mental welfare of the child would be adversely affected if travel documents were denied, or that a family crisis requires the child to travel urgently, **submit** full details to the Passport Office.

The consent must be witnessed by a person included in the categories eligible to complete the "Certification Regarding Applicant" listed in Section 11 below and cannot be a consenting party.

10. DECLARATION

Applicants should read the Declaration and ensure relevant sections of the form are complete and all supporting documents are attached before signing the Declaration.

If the applicant is a child who can sign his/her name then the child should sign the Declaration. If the child cannot sign, one parent/guardian only must sign the Declaration on the child's behalf.

11. CERTIFICATION REGARDING APPLICANT   No fee is chargeable for this certificate.

This certificate must be completed by a person **serving or practising** in one of the categories listed below, who should have known you and any children included in this application for at least 12 months and is not related by birth or marriage. If the application is lodged in Australia the person completing this certificate should be an Australian citizen. That person is also required to endorse one of your photographs as per instructions overleaf.

Members of Federal and State Parliament; Members of the House of Assembly of the ACT and the Legislative Assemblies of the Northern Territory and Norfolk Island; Aldermen and Councillors of Municipal and Shire Councils; Town Clerks and Shire Clerks/Secretaries; Medical Practitioners; Dentists; Pharmacists; Veterinary Surgeons; Barristers; Solicitors; Judges, Stipendiary Magistrates, Clerks of Petty Sessions, Clerks of Courts, Sheriffs, Bailiffs; Commissioned Offices of the Armed Services; Police Officers of the rank of Sergeant and above and Officers in charge of Stations; Ministers of Religion designated as authorised Marriage Celebrants; Full-time Teachers of at least five years service at schools and tertiary education institutions; Postmasters of Official Post Offices; Federal, State, Territory and Norfolk Island Public Servants of at least 10 years permanent service; Holders of statutory offices in respect of which an annual salary is payable.

Warning to witness and persons giving the certificate regarding applicant. Please ensure that you are within the categories listed above and that all blank spaces are struck through so that information cannot be added after you have signed the declaration. **Please note** that you may be contacted by the Passport Office for confirmation of this certification.

Department of Foreign Affairs
AUSTRALIAN PASSPORT APPLICATION

OFFICIAL USE ONLY

IMPORTANT: Before completing this application read the information notes and refer to the instructions opposite as you complete each section.
Answer all questions. If not applicable indicate "N/A".
Please use BLOCK CAPITALS with the exception of signatures.

1. NAME
SURNAME
GIVEN NAMES

If above differs from names at birth or on certificate of citizenship complete the following:

NAME AT BIRTH
NAME ON CERTIFICATE OF CITIZENSHIP

2. PERSONAL PARTICULARS

PLACE OF BIRTH — Suburb/Town — Country (optional if born outside Australia) — SEX (M or F)

DATE OF BIRTH — Day Month Year — HEIGHT cm

MOTHER'S MAIDEN SURNAME — HAVE YOU EVER BEEN MARRIED? Write YES or NO

3. UNMARRIED CHILDREN UNDER 18 YEARS OF AGE whose names you wish included in your passport

Surname	Given names	Town/City	Country (optional)	SEX M/F	Day	Month	Year

PLACE OF BIRTH / DATE OF BIRTH

— If space above is inadequate, attach a separate sheet giving this information for all children.

4. RESIDENTIAL ADDRESS

No. Street
Town/City   Postcode

NAME
RESIDENTIAL ADDRESS

Home Telephone — STD Code
Work Telephone — STD Code

Is Passport to be forwarded by certified mail? Write YES or NO

NAME AND ADDRESS LABEL

5. PREVIOUS AUSTRALIAN PASSPORT

(a) Have you or anyone included in Section 3 been issued an Australian Passport? Write YES or NO

If YES submit that passport and provide

Passport No.
Date of issue

(b) Has your previous Australian Passport issued in the last 5 years been lost, stolen or destroyed? Write YES or NO

If YES read instruction 5 and submit documentation

6. FOREIGN CITIZENSHIP

Do you or anyone included in Section 3 hold citizenship of another country? Write YES or NO

If YES complete the following

Country
Date acquired
How acquired

If you hold a current passport of that country submit it with this application and provide

Passport No.
Date of issue

7. SPECIMEN SIGNATURES

Sign both the specimen signature labels below using normal signature for inclusion in the passport. If the passport is for a child who is unable to sign, then write "UNABLE TO SIGN"

Please ensure your signatures are within the labels

PC1 (Jul 84)

THIS FORM IS ISSUED WITHOUT CHARGE

8. PERSON TO NOTIFY IN CASE OF EMERGENCY

Full name		Relationship	
Residential address		Home Telephone	STD Code
		Work Telephone	STD Code

9. CONSENT OF PARENTS/LEGAL GUARDIANS for children under 18 years of age (Place a cross ☒ in the appropriate box)

— This consent must be completed by all parents/guardians or persons having access to the child. Attach separate consents if applicable.
— The consent must be witnessed by a person within the categories listed in Section 11 of the instructions.

I/We **Full name of father/guardian** and **Full name of mother/guardian**

of **Address of father/guardian** **Address of mother/guardian**

hereby consent to
☐ the grant of a passport to my/our child named below
☐ the inclusion in a passport of my/our child/ren named below

1.	4.
2.	5.
3.	6.

Signature of father/guardian | Date | Signature of mother/guardian | Date

— The witness should read the notes in Section 11 of the instructions before completing.

I **Full name of witness** Occupation as per Section 11

of **Residential address** Home Telephone | STD Code
Work Telephone | STD Code

I hereby certify that the foregoing consent/s was/were **signed in my presence** and that to the best of my knowledge and belief the person/s who signed the same is/are the parent/guardian/s or person having legal access to the child/ren named above.

Signature of witness | Date

10. DECLARATION (Place a cross ☒ in the appropriate box)

I, the undersigned person making this
☐ application hereby declare that I am an Australian citizen, I understand that while travelling abroad I am subject to the laws of other countries and
☐ declaration on behalf of the applicant who cannot sign, hereby declare

that the statements made in this application are true and correct in every particular. I understand that under Section 10 of the Passports Act 1938, any person making a false or misleading statement whether orally or in writing, is liable to a penalty of two years imprisonment.

Signature of applicant | Date

11. CERTIFICATION REGARDING APPLICANT No fee is chargeable for this certificate

— The person giving this certificate should read the notes in Section 11 of the instructions before completing.

I **Full name** Occupation as per Section 11

Residential address **Business name and address**

Telephone | STD Code | Telephone | STD Code

hereby declare that I am an Australian citizen * and that I have known **Full name of applicant** personally for a period of ___ years.

To the best of my knowledge and belief the statements made by the applicant in this form are true and the signature on the application is that of the applicant. I have **endorsed the back of one of the accompanying photographs** of the applicant and his/her child/ren.
*May be deleted if application is lodged outside Australia.

Signature of person giving certification | Date

OFFICIAL USE ONLY   Receipt number/Cash register record

Interviewing/Certifying officer | Issue approved
/ / | / /

Who gets unemployment benefit?

Unemployment benefit is for people who are temporarily out of work.

You must be willing and able to work, and looking for a job.

You must be 16 or older (but under 65 for a man and under 60 for a woman).

You must have lived in Australia for at least a year, or intend to live here permanently.

If you are unable to support yourself and your dependants, and you cannot get unemployment benefit you may be able to get some other Social Security payment such as special benefit. Ask for more information at any Social Security office.

How you are paid

Payment is made by cheque every two weeks to your home address.

With your cheque will be an "Application for Continuation of Unemployment Benefit".

This form will have a date on it to show when you must post or take it back to Social Security.

You will not be paid any more benefit if you do not return this form.

You must remain registered for work with the CES and continue to look for work while receiving unemployment benefit.

You must also tell Social Security as soon as you get a job.

Note: From mid-1985 your benefit will be paid directly to your —
- bank account
- credit union savings account, or
- building society savings account.

However, the "Application for Continuation of Unemployment Benefit" form will still be sent to your home address and you will have to complete and return it to Social Security if you still want to get unemployment benefits.

Income tax

Unemployment benefit (but not guardian's allowance or extra payments for children) is taxable. How much tax you have to pay will depend on how much benefit and how much other income you get during the year.

The Department of Social Security will deduct tax from your benefit unless you fill in the Income Tax Instalment Declaration attached to the First Income Statement. If you wish, Social Security can arrange to have some tax taken from each benefit cheque.

Ask the Tax Office for help if you have any questions about tax. The Tax Office's telephone number is in the front of the telephone book under "Commonwealth Government".

Medicare

All Australian residents can get a Medicare card from Medicare. Your Medicare card entitles you to —

- free medical treatment if your doctor bulk-bills i.e. if he or she sends the bill to Medicare. If your doctor gives you the bill you can claim Medicare benefits from Medicare. These benefits amount to 85% of the "Schedule fee". The most you will have to pay is $10 for each service if your doctor charges the "Schedule fee". Some doctors charge more than the

"Schedule fee". In these cases you will have to make up the difference between the Medicare benefits refund and what the doctor charges. Similar cover applies to eye tests from optometrists.

- free accommodation and treatment, by a hospital doctor, in shared rooms of public hospitals. The card does not entitle you to treatment by a private doctor in hospital.
- free outpatient treatment at public hospitals.

For more information about Medicare call your nearest Medicare office or write to Medicare, GPO Box 9822 in your capital city.

Health Care card

You will automatically get a Health Care card if you are on unemployment benefit and your gross income (apart from benefits) is below the following levels.

	no children	with one child	add for each extra child
	$ a week	$ a week	$ a week
single	60	80	20
married (combined)	98	118	20

(Family allowance, family income supplement, orphan's pension and handicapped child's allowance do not count as income.)

If you do not get a card automatically because your income is above these levels, you can apply for a card as a low income earner. You will have to apply at a Social Security office.

The addresses and telephone numbers of Social Security offices are in the front of the telephone book under 'Commonwealth Government'.

DEPARTMENT OF SOCIAL SECURITY OFFICES ARE AT:

NSW
Metropolitan
Auburn
Bankstown
Belmore
Blacktown
Bondi Junction
Burwood
Campbelltown
Caringbah
Chatswood
Crows Nest
Darlinghurst
Dee Why
Fairfield
Hornsby
Hurstville
Liverpool
Manly
Maroubra
Marrickville
* Merrylands
Mt Druitt
* Newtown
Parramatta
Petersham
* Randwick
Redfern
Revesby
Rockdale
St Marys
Strathfield
* Sutherland
Sydney (City)
West Ryde

Country
Albury
Armidale
Bathurst
Bega
Broadmeadow
Broken Hill
* Byron Bay
* Cardiff
Cessnock
Charlestown
Coffs Harbour
* Corrimal
* Dapto
Dubbo
Gosford
Goulburn
Grafton
Griffith
Kempsey
Lismore
Lithgow
Maitland
Mayfield
Moree
Murwillumbah
Newcastle
Nowra
Orange
Penrith
Port Macquarie
* Queanbeyan
Tamworth
Taree
The Entrance
Wagga
Warilla
Warrawong
Windsor
Wollongong

VICTORIA
Metropolitan
Boronia
Box Hill
Camberwell
Caulfield
Cheltenham
Coburg
Footscray
Frankston
Glenroy
Greensborough
Heidelberg
Knox
Melbourne (City)
Moonee Ponds
North Fitzroy
Northcote
Oakleigh
Prahran
Preston
Richmond
Ringwood
St Kilda
Springvale
Sunshine
Werribee

Country
Ballarat
Belmont
Bendigo
Dandenong
Geelong
Hamilton
Horsham
Mildura
Morwell
Sale
Shepparton
Swan Hill
Wangaratta
Warrnambool
Wendouree

QUEENSLAND
Metropolitan
Alderley
Buranda
Chermside
Fortitude Valley
Inala
Indooroopilly
Mt Gravatt
Nundah
Stones Corner
Woodridge
Wynnum

Country
Aitkenvale
Bundaberg
Burleigh Heads
Cairns
Gladstone
Gympie
Ipswich
Mackay
Maroochydore
Maryborough
Mt Isa
Nambour
Redcliffe
Rockhampton
Southport
Toowoomba
Townsville
Warwick

SOUTH AUSTRALIA
Metropolitan
Adelaide (City)
Edwardstown
Elizabeth
Enfield
Gawler
Glenelg
Hawthorn
Marden
Modbury
Noarlunga
Norwood
Pt Adelaide
Salisbury
Torrensville
Woodville

Country
Berri
Kadina
Mt Gambier
Murray Bridge
Pt Augusta
Pt Lincoln
Pt Pirie
Whyalla

WESTERN AUSTRALIA
Metropolitan
Cannington
Causeway
Fremantle
Fremantle North
Innaloo
Midland
Mirrabooka
Morley
Perth East
Perth West
Rockingham
Victoria Park

Country
Albany
Broome
Bunbury
Carnarvon
Geraldton
Kalgoorlie
Kununurra
Mandurah
Northam
South Hedland

TASMANIA
Metropolitan
Bellerive
Glenorchy
Hobart (City)

Country
Burnie
Devonport
Launceston
Mowbray
Queenstown

A.C.T.
Canberra (Civic)
Belconnen
* Queanbeyan
Woden

NORTHERN TERRITORY
Metropolitan
Casuarina
Darwin

Country
Alice Springs
Katherine
Nhulunbuy
Tennant Creek

* Unemployment and sickness benefit offices

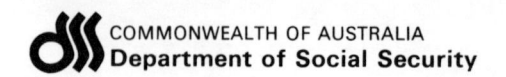

COMMONWEALTH OF AUSTRALIA
Department of Social Security

PROOF OF IDENTITY — ADVANCE ADVICE

Claimant's Name

- Please bring as many documents as you wish to help prove your identity.
- Documents from at least three different sources are preferred.
- If you have difficulty obtaining the documents, please let our counter staff know IMMEDIATELY. This will help avoid any delay in the payment.
- I will be able to bring an original

  - ☐ Birth Certificate
  - ☐ Birth Extract
  - ☐ Marriage Certificate
  - ☐ Australian Passport
  - ☐ Overseas Passport
  - ☐ Entry Visa
  - ☐ Refugee documents
  - ☐ Citizenship papers
  - ☐ Tax Assessment
  - ☐ Group Certificate
  - ☐ School Report
  - ☐ Insurance Policy
  - ☐ Drivers licence showing current address
  - ☐ Credit Card
  - ☐ Membership of a medical fund
  - ☐ Membership of a motoring organisation
  - ☐ Trade/Apprenticeship documents
  - ☐ Trade Union membership
  - ☐ Other documents *(please specify)* _____
    _____
    _____
    _____
    _____
    _____

Proof of identity—advance advice form.

SS207.8410

COMMONWEALTH OF AUSTRALIA
Department of Social Security

CLAIM FOR UNEMPLOYMENT BENEFIT

A brief guide on how to claim Unemployment Benefit is on the next page. If you want to know more, a leaflet is available from offices of the Department of Social Security, the Commonwealth Employment Service, or post offices.

The leaflet and the notes on the next page are a guide only. If you want more information contact the office of the Department of Social Security nearest you. The offices are listed in the telephone directory.

If you cannot answer a question or do not have all the information required you should not delay making your claim. Note in the space by the question that you do not have all the information, and return the form. Social Security staff will help where necessary.

TURKISH Eğer bu formu doldurmak için kendi dilinizde yardıma ihtiyacınız varsa, size en yakın Sosyal Güvenlik Bakanlığı Şubesine Getiriniz. Eğer o şubede Türkçe bilen yoksa, telefon tercüme servisinde bir tercümanla konuşmanız sağlanacaktır.	**SPANISH** Si necesita ayuda en su propio idioma para completar esto, por favor llévelo a la Oficina del Departamento de la Seguridad Social más cercana. Si en esa oficina no hay nadie que hable español, usted podrá comunicarse con un intérprete a través del Servicio Telefónico de Intérpretes.
ITALIAN Se vi serve aiuto nella vostra lingua per completare questo, per piacere portatelo al più vicino ufficio della Previdenza Sociale (Department of Social Security). Se non c'é nessuno in questo ufficio che parla l'Italiano, lei potra parlare con un interprete attraverso il Servizio Telefonico di Interpreti.	**GREEK** Αν χρειάζεστε βοήθεια γιά νά συμπληρώσετε τήν αίτηση αὐτή στή γλώσσα-σας, σάς παρακαλούμε νά ἀποταθῆτε στό πλησιέστερο γραφείο τοῦ Ὑπουργείου Κοινωνικῶν Ἀσφαλίσεων. Ἄν τό γραφείο στό ὁποίο ἀποταθήκατε δέν διαθέτει ὑπάλληλο πού νά μιλά ἑλληνικά, ἡ ἐξυπηρέτησή-σας μπορεί τότε νά γίνει τηλεφωνικά μέ τήν Τηλεφωνική Ὑπηρεσία Διερμηνέων.
VIETNAMESE Nếu bạn cần người nói được Tiếng Việt giúp bạn làm giấy tờ này thì mời bạn mang giấy tờ này đến cơ quan của Bộ Xã Hội gần nhất. Các người đó rất vui lòng giúp bạn. Nếu không có người nói được tiếng Việt nam thì họ có thể dùng thông dịch bằng điện thoại để giúp bạn.	**CROATIAN** Ako trebate pomoći u vašem jeziku, kompletno da uspunite ovo, dodite u najbližu kancelariju Socijalne Sluzbe, a ako nijsmo u mogućnosti da vam obezbjedimo tumaća, moći će te se konsultovati sa tumaćem preko Telefonske Prevodilaćke Sluzbe.
SERBIAN У случају да вам треба помоћ да ово испуните обратите се најближем уреду Социјалне безбедности. Ако немамо Српског Тумача на располужењу онда можете да говорите са тумачем преко Телефонске Преводилачке Службе.	**ARABIC** اذا احتجت مساعدة لتعبئة هذه الاستمارة بـالغة العربية، فالرجاء احضارها الى اقرب مكتب لدائرة الضمان الاجتماعي. اذا لم يكن لدينا احد في ذلك المكتب متكلم للعربية ستستطيع التحدث الى مترجم عن طريق مكتب خدمة الترجمة التليفونية.

A guide to claiming unemployment benefits in Australia.

**PLEASE READ THE NOTES BEFORE YOU FILL IN THE FORM.
YOU CAN TEAR OUT AND KEEP THIS PAGE.**

WHO CAN CLAIM?
To be paid unemployment benefit you must:
- be unemployed
- be able to work and willing to work
- must have taken reasonable steps to obtain work
- not be studying a course which stops you working full-time
- not be unemployed due to industrial action by yourself or by a union of which you are a member
- not be getting an age, wife's, invalid or widow's pension, a supporting parent's benefit, an allowance under the National Employment and Training Scheme, some forms of State Government aid, a TB allowance, or a service pension (you can be getting a war pension however)
- be at least 16 years of age. Men must be under 65 years of age, and women under 60 years.
- have lived continuously in Australia for at least one year before you claim, or intend to live here permanently.

OTHER BENEFITS
If you cannot get unemployment benefit you may be able to claim other forms of benefit such as sickness benefit if you are ill, or special benefit if you are in need. You should ask at your nearest Department of Social Security office if you think you may be eligible.

IF YOU ARE MARRIED
A married person can be paid unemployment benefit if he or she becomes unemployed, but any income or any age, invalid, wife's or widow's pension or other benefits received by his or her partner is taken into account. This can affect how much benefit is paid.

For benefit purposes, a couple living together in a 'de facto' relationship are treated in the same way as a married couple. On the claim form, the term 'husband' covers a 'de facto husband', and the term 'wife' covers a 'de facto wife'.

OTHER GOVERNMENT ASSISTANCE
This includes an invalid, age or wife's pension, a widow's pension, a supporting parent's benefit, a tuberculosis allowance, assistance from a state social welfare department, an allowance under the Tertiary Education Assistance Scheme (TEAS), National Employment and Training Scheme (NEATS) or similar schemes.

IF YOU HAVE INCOME
How much income a person or his or her partner has can affect how much unemployment benefit may be paid.

Income includes:
- earnings, sick or holiday pay, sickness or accident insurance, compensation, superannuation, retiring allowance or similar payments, long service leave payments.
- bank interest, net profits from shops or businesses, interest on mortgage loans or bonds, dividends from shares or debentures, royalties.
- regular gifts or allowances, an annuity or income from a deceased estate, maintenance or alimony.
- overseas pension, miner's pension.
- income from rent or from boarders, the value of free board, or board in return for services.

Income does not include family allowances or other payments for children, or health insurance benefits. Payment from Army, Air or Navy Reserve service does not affect benefit.

HOW DO YOU CLAIM?
If you wish to claim Unemployment Benefit you must first register with the Commonwealth Employment Service (C.E.S.). The C.E.S. will tell you where you should lodge your claim form when you have completed it. This will normally be at your nearest Department of Social Security office.

PROOF OF IDENTITY
When you lodge the form, it would help if you could provide proof of identity such as a birth or marriage certificate, tax assessment notice for last year, or a passport (not a driver's licence). However, if this is not possible, do not delay lodgement of the form. Proof of identity can be provided later.

HOW TO COMPLETE THE FORM
- read the form through before you start to fill it in.
- answer all the questions you can.
- tick the box for a YES or NO answer.
- use pen not pencil.
- please do not use strokes or dashes.
- some questions apply to you and to your wife or husband. If you are married or living in a de facto relationship, please fill in both columns.

IF YOU WANT TO KNOW MORE ABOUT UNEMPLOYMENT BENEFIT OR NEED HELP TO FILL IN THE FORM, CONTACT YOUR LOCAL DEPARTMENT OF SOCIAL SECURITY OFFICE.

MAXIMUM PENALTY FOR A DELIBERATE FALSE DECLARATION IS $500 OR SIX MONTHS IMPRISONMENT

Claim for Unemployment Benefit

COMMONWEALTH OF AUSTRALIA
Department of Social Security

- Read the Notes attached before completing this claim form.
- The Commonwealth Employment Service will tell you where to return this form.

OFFICE USE ONLY

11 Benefit Number

Tfr Sp CES Office

Date of Reg.
Notional D.O.L.

CES Date of Issue

DSS Date of Receipt

Date of Registration

WT applied and NSWA

POI supplied? YES / NO
Documents:

DSS Office referred to

Batch No.

Prepared by:

Date

Cross Reference Number

YOUR FULL NAME
(1) ☐ Mr   (3) ☐ Miss
(2) ☐ Mrs (4) ☐ Ms
Surname (Family Name)
First Christian or Given Name | Other Names | Sex (M or F)

YOUR POSTAL ADDRESS — U1
No. | Street
Suburb or Town | Postcode

Your Date of Birth: Day | Month | Year
Your Place of Birth
Your Telephone No.

YOUR RESIDENTIAL ADDRESS — U2
If same as postal address, write 'as above'.
No. | Street
Suburb or Town | Postcode

YOUR PARENTS' NAMES
Father's Name
Mother's Name

Are you:
☐ married and living together   ☐ separated   ☐ widowed
☐ living with another person as husband & wife on a de facto basis   ☐ single   ☐ divorced

If you tick one of these boxes, you must complete the following section.
For benefit purposes, a man & woman living together as husband & wife on a bona fide domestic basis (i.e. on a de facto basis), although not legally married, are treated in the same way as a legally married couple who live together.

FULL NAME OF YOUR WIFE OR HUSBAND — U3
Surname (Family Name)
First Christian or Given Name | Other Names

Date of Birth of Your Wife or Husband: Day | Month | Year
Wife's Maiden Name

DEPENDANTS

I have the custody, care and control, or contribute to the maintenance of the following children or dependants.

CHILDREN, UNDER 16 YEARS, IN ORDER OF AGE (ELDEST FIRST)

Surname	Christian or Given Names	My relationship to child	Date of Birth (Day/Mth/Yr)	Place of Birth (Suburb or Town, and State, Territory or Country)	Is the child living with you?

DEPENDANTS WHO ARE FULL-TIME STUDENTS, AGED 16 – 24 YEARS (ELDEST FIRST)

Surname	Christian or Given Names	My relationship to student	Date of Birth (Day/Mth/Yr)	Name of School, College or University	Is the student living with you?

SU 2 (Mar 81)   **QUESTIONS CONTINUE ▶**

#			
1	Have you lived in Australia for the last twelve months?	☐ YES ☐ NO	
	If NO, do you intend to live in Australia permanently?	☐ YES ☐ NO	
2	If you are under 18 years of age, do either of your parents live in Australia?	☐ YES ☐ NO	
3	Are you doing a course of study?	☐ YES ☐ NO	
4	Have you stopped studying recently?	☐ YES ☐ NO	
	If YES, state date you stopped	/ /	
5	If you are studying or have recently stopped studying, state:		
	(a) name of institution		
	(b) title of course		
	(c) whether part-time or full-time		
6	On what date did you last work?	/ /	
7	Give the name and address of your last employer:		

8 Why did you stop work?

9 Were you self-employed? ☐ YES ☐ NO

10 What is your usual occupation (job)?

11 When did you start looking for another job? / /

12 What attempts have you made to find new work? Give the names and addresses of the places where you tried.

Please answer the following questions about 'YOURSELF'.
CLAIMANTS who are MARRIED or living in a DE FACTO relationship must also answer about 'YOUR WIFE OR HUSBAND'.

#		YOURSELF	YOUR WIFE OR HUSBAND
13	Have you previously claimed unemployment, special or sickness benefit?	☐ YES ☐ NO	☐ YES ☐ NO
	If YES, state: (a) when you last applied		
	(b) where you applied		
	(c) when you were last paid		
	(d) your address when you were last paid		
14	Do you receive or have you recently applied for assistance from the Dept. of Veterans' Affairs (including a war pension)?	☐ YES ☐ NO	☐ YES ☐ NO
	If YES, state: (a) type of assistance		
	(b) rate paid per fortnight	$	$
15	Do you receive or have you recently applied for any other form of Government assistance?	☐ YES ☐ NO	☐ YES ☐ NO
	If YES, state: (a) type of assistance		
	(b) rate paid per fortnight.	$	$
16	Are you employed (including casual work)?	☐ YES ☐ NO	☐ YES ☐ NO
	If YES, state weekly wages (before tax)	$	$
17	Do you have bank, credit union or building society accounts?	☐ YES ☐ NO	☐ YES ☐ NO
	If YES, state: TYPE OF ACCOUNT	IN NAME(S) OF	AMOUNT DEPOSITED · INTEREST RATE
18	Do you receive or are you entitled to receive any income from any other source? (see Notes)	☐ YES ☐ NO	☐ YES ☐ NO
	If YES, state:	SOURCE · WEEKLY AMOUNT (before tax)	SOURCE · WEEKLY AMOUNT (before tax)

STATEMENT

I claim unemployment benefit and declare that:
(a) I am unemployed
(b) I am capable of undertaking and willing to undertake work
(c) I have taken all reasonable steps to obtain employment since I became unemployed
(d) to the best of my knowledge and belief, all the information furnished in this claim is true and correct.

I authorise the Department of Social Security to make any enquiries necessary to determine my entitlement to benefit.

PLEASE SIGN HERE

Signature ....

Date ..../........../..........

Maximum penalty for a deliberate false declaration is $500 or 6 months imprisonment.

lia for a period of fourteen days to three months, and can even be put into use within six months of the date of issue. This delay may prove very useful to certain persons who are hoping to throw potential followers off their scent!

The Austrailpass can be purchased from Thomas Cook offices in North America, New Zealand, Europe, and the United Kingdom. Check with them for current prices. You will probably find out about other companies offering travel passes from local travel agents. Note that some passes carry a photo of the holder, while others do not.

NOTE: At the time of writing, the Australian government was considering the introduction of a national I.D. document. Be sure to look into its existence before you decide to acquire I.D. in Australia.

---

3. NEW ZEALAND

At present, no cross-referencing of birth and death records is undertaken in New Zealand. This situation is unlikely to change in the near future since, except for passports, false I.D. procurement is not nearly as serious a problem in New Zealand as it is in other countries.

BIRTH CERTIFICATE

As in the other countries covered in this book, birth certificates may be obtained in New Zealand by researching details of deaths in libraries and church records, and applying for a duplicate certificate using information obtained therefrom.

Acquiring Necessary Information

Apart from the methods previously mentioned and searching through death records held by registry offices, there is yet another technique for securing pertinent birth details that has been used in the past with excellent results. This technique primarily relies on being in the right place at the right time.

Quite simply, closely watch the local newspapers and listen to radio stations for mention of deaths by accident, disaster, or even natural causes (although of the three categories, death by natural causes is the less frequently reported on the radio). Once a suitable candidate is reported as having died, set about securing information relating to that person's parents, date of birth, etc., in order to obtain a birth certificate in his or her name. Finding out such details is not difficult, but does entail considerable motivation and ability. The technique is to contact the deceased's friends, relatives, workmates, or neighbors and tactfully elicit the required information under the guise of being a reporter from a different media. Should you use this method, explain that you are a freelance reporter and do not claim to work for any specific paper or radio station. Most friends and relatives will agree to talk to you, especially if you imply that by doing so they will help to prevent "similar accidents," senseless deaths, etc. Hard as it sounds, it will also be found that if such a person is approached within a few hours of the tragedy, he will be so shocked at the death that he will not really be aware of what you are asking or what he is saying. Show a lot of sympathy and disguise the relevant questions with more general ones.

Local radio stations often broadcast news of auto wrecks or other accidents within an hour of their occurrence, getting much of their information by monitoring police, ambulance, and fire-service transmissions on scanning receivers. These useful radios can be purchased quite cheaply from Radio Shack outlets, and are well worth the investment if you want to be among the first on the scene.

As soon as you hear a suitable report, head off to the appropriate location and start your freelance reporter act. You will probably find that there are several legitimate journalists from other radio stations or newspapers already on the scene, and conducting a few tactful inquiries may also provide you with some useful details. If you are the sort of person who hates to hassle others, especially when they are obviously distressed, this is not the technique for you. I do a fair bit of freelance work, including some photography, and I know that this technique is workable. You do, though, need to be somewhat hardhearted.

The only word of caution I will give you here is that you should not use the name of a victim who has died in such an unusual manner that his name will be remembered by listeners or readers for some time. Similarly, a person whose death has been reported nationally should be ignored. Stick to low-key, local media sources, or monitor the emergency services yourself. Sometimes, monitoring such frequencies will provide enough information for you to apply for a certificate, anyway.

It is obvious that this technique or its variations will provide sufficient details concerning a deceased *adult* so that you can secure a birth certificate in his or her name. You may then assume the identity of that person. If you are concerned that negative information about him may have been generated during his lifetime, or if you intend to apply for a passport in that name and need to confirm whether he had been issued a passport, ensure that you obtain additional background information. As an example of how such information may be easily secured without asking questions outright, study the way in which genuine news reporters get interviewees to open up on a range of subjects without having to ask a lot of questions. (For example, one question you can ask is, "Was he planning to travel abroad again this year?" The question can provoke a range of answers which would indicate whether or not the person had a passport, and yet no mention of a passport has been made in the question.)

As previously mentioned, birth and death records are not cross-referenced in New Zealand and, although there is a simple application form to be completed by persons seeking copies, if you apply by mail (giving as many details as possible), even this process can be avoided. If you do apply in person, there is no identification requirement. If, however, you are claiming to be a citizen seeking a certificate for your own use, practice your accent first!

Oh, yes, don't be too put off by the fact that the phone number for the registry office in Wellington, New Zealand, is listed under the Justice Department! I have it on good authority that the staff there is very helpful indeed.

PASSPORT

Photos, a declaration by a referee, and presentation of a birth certificate, as well as other information is required in New Zealand in order to obtain a passport. The application form is reproduced herein and shows clearly what the precise requirements are.

Research indicates that New Zealand has had some problems with persons trying to secure passports and other items of identification. Note the reference to the 1980 Passport Act in the warning square.

An important factor to consider while filling in this application is that the identification certificate (statement by the referee) may be signed by *anyone* over the age of eighteen who has known the applicant for twelve months or longer. It is interesting to note that the New Zealand authorities do not stipulate that the referee be a lawyer, magistrate, doctor, or of a particular occupation. This lack of specificity obviously makes it easier for one to provide the required statement.

Verification checks of applicants are not made as a matter of course. If the birth certificate is genuine—and it will be if you follow the techniques shown herein—you will be issued the passport within a couple of weeks. As always, the best time to apply is during peak holiday periods when the processing officers will be extremely busy and not have time to cross-check any but the most apparent of attempted frauds.

DRIVER'S LICENSE

New Zealand laws do not require that someone who is learning to drive obtain a provisional license; such a person must, however, be accompanied on the road by a qualified driver. To get a driver's license, a New Zealand citizen must produce a birth certificate, while noncitizens must show either a birth certificate or passport. The test itself consists of four parts: eyesight and hearing, written, oral, and practical sections. It is permissible to show a doctor's certificate which states that your eyesight and hearing are in order.

The written test consists of twenty-five questions taken from the *Road Code* and the *Standard Driving Test Questionnaire*. Both these documents are available free of charge from post offices or the Local Body Traffic Department. However, in case you intend to study for the test out of the country, the actual test questions and answers are reprinted on the following pages. It can be seen that there are five sets of twenty-five questions. On the test you will only have to answer, in written form, a *total* of twenty-five. To pass the test, you must answer at least twenty-three correctly, including five of the last six! The oral test consists of five questions concerning equipment or use of the vehicle for which you desire a license; at least four of these must be answered correctly.

The *Road Code* covers all aspects of driving in New Zealand that are not included in the driving-test information booklet. If you intend to apply for the test, pick a copy up once you get in the country and study it *before* applying.

As you can see in the introduction section of the *Written Driving Test* form, a birth certificate is required of all persons seeking a license for the first time. This is not part of an antighost policy, but results from the New Zealand driving laws which allow persons of different ages to obtain different types of licenses. For example, a fifteen-year-old may apply for a license to drive a private car, motorcycle, light vehicle or forklift, and certain weights of tractors. However, the applicant must be at least eighteen years old if he wants a license to drive heavy trade vehicles, special vehicles above specified weights, and heavy tractors. A license to drive a taxi, bus, trolley bus, or passenger service vehicle will only be issued to persons of twenty years of age or above.

At the risk of repeating myself, I will remind you here that if you apply for a license issued by a country other than your own using the identity of a local citizen, always study for the test as if you were learning to drive for the first time. (I assume that most of you drive already.) The differences in test technique and knowledge requirements among countries which apparently seem to be very similar are in actuality greater than you may think.

SOCIAL SECURITY NUMBER

For those of you who are used to the American system of Social Security numbers, it might come as a surprise to learn that the system in New Zealand is very different indeed. Social Security numbers and cards are not issued as a matter of course, but are reserved instead for persons claiming certain forms of government assistance.

It then follows that in the context of identification, a Social Security number in New Zealand does not really exist. As in the Australian system, persons seeking assistance from the social welfare department must prove their identity to the satisfaction of staff dealing with the claim, by supplying a birth certificate, passport, or other suitable "piece of paper."

As in Australia and England, there is no national identity document in New Zealand, and the absence of a Social Security number means that a wide range of identification will be accepted by various authorities, depending on what you are trying to prove and to whom. (See the Australian section on what identification the social security department there considers acceptable and you will get an idea of how flexible such systems are.)

MEDICAL CARD

There is no "free" national health service as such in New Zealand, although fees payable to a doctor who treats a patient for backache, for example, are heavily subsidized by the government. The funds for this service are generated from general taxation. New Zealand has such a comprehensive accident insurance policy that citizens *or visitors* who are injured accidentally—in any situation and regardless of fault—are entitled to compensation as well as free medical treatment. The compensation is a right, and is never subject to legal wrangling. This being the case, the government has decided that no one may bring a private action for damages before the courts. The right to do so has been removed!

Because of New Zealand's comprehensive accident insurance system and the subsidization of hospital or medical costs, the authorities do not issue a medical card (as used in England to establish an individual's right to treatment). Useful identification could be obtained by registering with a doctor and obtaining an appointment card or other similar paperwork. If treatment is sought, the prescription(s) would be adequate supportive identification in a variety of situations since it indicates one's name.

A blank medical identification card, which lists any details that may be important if you are involved in an accident (blood type, allergy to penicillin, for example) can be obtained and completed by the holder. A blank can also be purchased from various international travel groups which will print the details you provide onto a more impressive card or plastic form. Such cards carry considerable weight as few (sensible) people would risk carrying fake details. For more details concerning medical matters as they may pertain to your visit or journey, contact the International Association for Medical Assistance to Traveler, 736 Center St., Lewiston, NY 14092, asking for information about insurance and the like, and Intermedic, 777 Third Avenue, New York, NY 10017. Be sure, though, to use the "right" name!

TRAVEL PASSES

New Zealand Railways offer off-season passes for tourists (April to December) at very reasonable

DEPARTMENT OF INTERNAL AFFAIRS

APPLICATION FOR NEW ZEALAND PASSPORT
FEE $30

1. PLEASE READ THE INFORMATION SHEET CAREFULLY BEFORE COMPLETING BOTH SIDES OF THE APPLICATION FORM. NOTE PARTICULARLY THE WARNING ABOUT MAKING FALSE STATEMENTS.

2. LIFE OF PASSPORT: A New Zealand passport has a total life of ten years from date of issue.

3. 21 DAYS NOTICE is normally required for processing an application. You should allow extra time if visas are required, or if your New Zealand citizenship has to be established. All requests for urgent issue must be by prior arrangement with the Passport Officer. Passport fees may not be paid by cheque if departure date is within 10 days.

4. VISAS: Your travel agent will advise you for which countries visas are required. *Do not send applications for visas with your passport application.* Visa applications should be sent with your passport, to the Embassy of the country concerned.

5. DOCUMENTARY EVIDENCE
    (a) *Documents:* All documents are returned. A document that is illegible, torn or has been altered will not be accepted.
    (b) *Photocopies of Documents are not acceptable.*
    (c) *New Zealand Passport:* A previous New Zealand passport (issued after 1 January 1950) may be submitted as evidence of citizenship and name. The passport will be cancelled and returned with your new passport.

6. NEW ZEALAND CITIZENSHIP (BLOCK 6)

    New Zealand passports may only be issued to New Zealand citizens. Before a New Zealand passport can be issued, the applicant's claim to New Zealand citizenship must be established:

    (a) *Birth in New Zealand (including Cook Islands, Niue, Tokelau).* Please forward your birth certificate. A full birth certificate is preferred (RG 100 or RG 3G Certified Copy of Entry of Birth) and is compulsory for children under 16 years of age.

    (b) *British subject by birth, and ordinarily resident in New Zealand throughout the whole of 1948* — A Statutory Declaration on a form available from the Passport Office must be made before a Justice of the Peace, a solicitor, postmaster, or a Government officer duly authorised.

    (c) *Grant of New Zealand Citizenship* — please give details of Register and Page No. and if possible forward your certificate.

    (d) *By descent* —
        (i) If you were were not born in New Zealand, but have a parent who was a New Zealand citizen at the time of your birth contact your Passport Officer, who will advise what documents are required. Generally, full birth certificate and marriage certificates are required that clearly trace the line of descent.
        (ii) The New Zealand citizenship of a child born outside New Zealand after 1 January 1978 will lapse at age 22 if the birth is not registered. Enquire at the Department of Internal Affairs or, if overseas, at a New Zealand Consular Office.

7. HEIGHT — The following chart is provided to assist you to show the height of the passport holder in metrics. If in doubt *(e.g. babies and children)* please show in feet and inches and Passport Office will convert to metrics.

Ft.	Ins	Metres	Ft.	Ins.	Metres	Ft.	Ins.	Metres	Ft.	Ins.	Metres	Ft.	Ins.	Metres	Ft.	Ins.	Metres
4	6	1.37	4	10	1.47	5	2	1.57	5	6	1.68	5	10	1.78	6	2	1.88
4	7	1.40	4	11	1.50	5	3	1.60	5	7	1.70	5	11	1.80	6	3	1.91
4	8	1.42	5	0	1.52	5	4	1.63	5	8	1.73	6	0	1.83	6	4	1.93
4	9	1.45	5	1	1.55	5	5	1.65	5	9	1.75	6	1	1.85	6	5	1.96

8. CHANGE OF NAME (BLOCK 3) — NOTE: All changes of name must be shown and documentary evidence produced.
    (a) Passports are normally issued in the names recorded on the birth certificate.
    (b) Married women should state maiden name, and place and date of marriage(s), and enclose marriage certificate(s) to support each change of name. (RG 118 Copy of Entry of Marriage states bride's maiden name, and can be produced for the last marriage without any other marriage certificates being produced).
    (c) If you are a woman about to marry, your passport will be issued in your maiden name. Later you may have your married name endorsed in your passport.
    (d) If you have married since your passport was issued and it is still valid, your passport may be endorsed with your married name *(separate Endorsement Application Form).*
    (e) A married women may have her passport issued in her maiden name by providing evidence that the name is used for all purposes. The marriage details must be declared. Application must be signed and identification completed in the maiden name.
    (f) If your name has been changed other than by marriage, deed poll documents should be submitted. The passport officer can advise.

Application for a New Zealand passport.

9. CHILDREN (BLOCK 4 and BLOCK 8)

    Parental Consent
    (a) Full birth certificates (RG 100 or RG 3G Certified Copy of Entry of Birth) naming parents are required.
    (b) Children under the age of 16 years may be included on one or both parents' passports, or children may have separate passports.
    (c) In all cases the consent of one parent or the legal guardian is required.
    (d) A Court order or agreement concerning guardianship, or custody of, or access to a child does not necessarily prevent the issue of a passport, but attention is drawn to section 20 of the Guardianship Amendment Act 1979 which in certain circumstances requires that the Court's approval be obtained before a child may be taken out of New Zealand. The Court may order the surrender of all travel documents, including the passport. Persons resident/travelling overseas, including children born overseas, are reminded that they are subject to local law.

    NOTES— (1) Photographs of children to be included in a parent's passport are not required.
    (2) Children included in a parent's passport may not travel without the passport holder.
    (3) On reaching the age of 16 years a child requires a separate passport.
    (4) A legal guardian must provide documentary evidence of guardianship.
    (5) A child 10 years or over must sign his/her own application.

10. PREVIOUS NEW ZEALAND PASSPORTS HELD (BLOCK 7): You must declare details of all passports held, whether valid or not. All non-cancelled passports should be forwarded for cancellation, but will be returned to you. (See also 5—Documentary Evidence.)

11. LOST PASSPORTS (BLOCK 7): The loss of a passport is a serious matter and must be reported immediately to the nearest Passport Office. Theft of a passport should also be reported to the police. The replacement passport will have limited validity initially but can be extended without further fee.

12. PHOTOGRAPHS: Please enclose with your application **two identical** unmounted photographs, taken not more than one year before the date of your application.

    Please note that:
    (a) Photographs from a coin-operated vending machine are not acceptable.
    (b) Photographs may be black and white, or coloured, but must not be re-touched or hand-coloured. Prints must be sharp.
    (c) Photographs should be full-face, head and shoulders only, head uncovered, and against a plain background. The head must occupy a large part of the photograph.
    (d) Photographs must be within the following dimensions:
        depth — maximum 65mm, minimum 45mm.
        width — maximum 55mm, minimum 35mm.
    (e) The photograph must be a good likeness. This is for your protection while travelling.

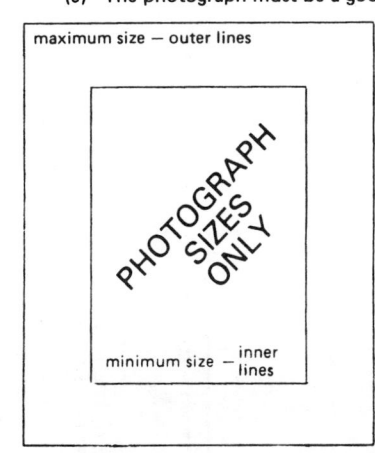

    (f) CERTIFYING PHOTOGRAPH: In order to identify you, one photograph must be certified on the back exactly as shown here, **by the same person who completes Block 9 on the application.**
    (The applicant must not complete any details for himself or herself).

13. IDENTIFICATION CERTIFICATE (BLOCK 9): Applicants must not complete any part of the section themselves. Identification is to be made by a person over the age of 18 years who has known you for at least 12 months, and who is not a relative. The person completing this section must be the same person certifying your photographs, **who should in his/her own handwriting complete all details on the form and on the back of the photograph.**

14. BEFORE POSTING *(See Addresses on reverse of application)* check carefully that all information required has been provided. Ensure that you have signed the application (see Block 10) and enclose all documents and the correct fee. All applicants 10 years and over must sign their own applications.

15. EMERGENCY ADDRESS (BLOCK 11): This section is included at the request of the Ministry of Foreign Affairs, and is for your protection should an emergency arise while you are overseas. It should be next-of-kin or close relative.

16. COLLECTION OF PASSPORTS: Any person collecting a passport on behalf of the applicant must state their relationship to the applicant and be able to identify themselves.

17. Please detach and retain this Information Sheet in the event of any query. Record your remittance and the date of despatch. Receipts are not generally issued for cheques.

    Date posted .... Fee paid .... Cash/Cheque/Postal Note.

APPLICATION FOR A NEW ZEALAND PASSPORT

FOR OFFICIAL USE ONLY

(Passport Number)

Fee Received: $............................
Cash/PN/M.O/Chq ....
Receipt No. ....
Received on ....
S/L checked by: .... on ....
Made up by: .... on ....
Final Check by: .... on ....
Posted on ....
Endorsements:

(Place and date of issue)

WARNING

Every person commits an offence against the Passport Act 1980, who for the purpose of procuring anything to be done or not to be done under any of the particular sections of the Act, whether for his own benefit or for the benefit of any other person, makes a statement that he knows to be false in a material particular, or recklessly makes a statement that is false in a material particular.

---

1 I am leaving on .... *(date)* from .... *(international airport/seaport)*
for .... *(country of destination)*

Particulars to appear in passport are as follows: (to be completed in applicants own handwriting).

PLEASE PRINT CLEARLY

2 SURNAME: ....
FORENAMES: ....
BIRTHPLACE: .... *(city/town)* .... *(country)*
BIRTHDATE: .... *(day)* .... *(month)* .... *(year)* SEX: ....
*HEIGHT: .... *(metres)* COLOUR OF EYES: ....
VISIBLE DISTINGUISHING CHARACTERISTICS: ....

(*See Information Note 7) Checked: .... on: ....

3 IF NAME HAS BEEN CHANGED SINCE BIRTH: (See Information Note 8)
(1st Change)   (2nd Change)   (3rd Change)
From ....
To ....
By .... *(e.g. marriage)*
At .... *(place)*
On .... *(date)*

4 CHILDREN under 16 years of age to be included in my passport whose full birth certificates are enclosed. Parental consent Block 8 has been completed. (See Information Note 9)

Surname	Forenames	Date of Birth	Place of Birth	Sex	Relationship to Applicant

5 ADDRESSES (a) residential (not Box No.) ....
(b) for dispatch of passport (post/collect): ....
(If Box No. given, State name of boxholder)
Telephone numbers — Home: .... Business: ....

---

6 **N.Z. CITIZENSHIP** (See Information Note 6)

I believe myself to be a New Zealand citizen by:

(Please tick where applicable)

☐ (a) Birth in New Zealand. Birth certificate is enclosed
☐ (b) British birth and residence in New Zealand throughout 1948. I enclose evidence of residence and birth certificate.
☐ (c) Grant of New Zealand Citizenship. Evidence is enclosed Register No. .... Page No. .... Date: ....
☐ (d) Descent. Documentary evidence enclosed.
☐ (e) Previous New Zealand Passport, which is enclosed.
☐ (f) Other reasons. A letter is attached detailing claim.

7 PREVIOUS NEW ZEALAND PASSPORTS HELD. If never held, tick here ☐
(See Information Notes 10 and 11)
Passport number .... issued at ....
on .... in the name of ....
This passport: ☐ is enclosed   ☐ is not enclosed
In the case of loss or theft, have Police been advised? ☐ YES ☐ NO
A separate report about the non-availability of any passport is required. Special forms are available from the Passport Office.

OFFICE USE: H.O. advised ☐

Applicant/or Relationship to Applicant ....
.... *(Signature)*
Date ....

POST | **COLLECT**

TO BE COMPLETED AT TIME PASSPORT COLLECTED

Collected By ....
Print Name ....

PAS 1

THE COMPLETED APPLICATION SHOULD BE SENT TO THE NEAREST PASSPORT OFFICE OF THE

DEPARTMENT OF INTERNAL AFFAIRS

at: AUCKLAND (P.O. Box 2220)
4th Floor, T. & G. Building
17 Albert Street,
Phone 31 184

or: ROTORUA (P.O. Box 1146)
2nd Floor, Government Building
Haupapa Street,
Phone 477 680

or: WELLINGTON (Private Bag)
2nd Floor, Local Government Building,
114–118 Lambton Quay,
Phone 738 699

or: CHRISTCHURCH (P.O. Box 1308)
M.L.C. No. 2 Building
159 Manchester Street,
Phone 790 290

or: DUNEDIN (P.O. Box 927)
2nd Floor, Public Trust Building,
442 Moray Place,
Phone 771 274

(Office hours for above are 9 a.m. to 4 p.m. Monday to Friday)

OVERSEAS APPLICANTS SHOULD SEND APPLICATIONS TO THE NEAREST NEW ZEALAND CONSULAR OFFICE OR TO THE DEPARTMENT OF INTERNAL AFFAIRS, PRIVATE BAG, WELLINGTON.

6751C—400,000/10/83MK

---

8 CONSENT OF PARENT OR GUARDIAN FOR CHILDREN UNDER 16 YEARS OF AGE (See Information Note 4)

The existence of a Court Order relating to custody does not necessarily prevent the issue of passport facilities, but correct information must be given. (See Warning overleaf)

I consent to the issue of a separate passport, or to the inclusion in the passport of .... of the child(ren) named hereinafter.
(Name of passport holder)

Full name of parent giving consent .... Phone No.: .... Relationship to child: | MOTHER | FATHER |
(Children's full names) Signature: ....

Address: ....
(NOTE: If consent is given by a legal guardian, documentary evidence of guardianship must be forwarded.)

ALL APPLICANTS MUST ANSWER Question (a), and if a custody order is in force or pending questions (b), (c) and (d) must also be answered

(a) Has any Order of any Court concerning the custody or guardianship of any child named above been issued or is an application for custody or access pending? | YES | NO |

(b) If YES, what is the name, address and phone number of the other parent? ....

(c) Is he/she aware that application has been made for passport facilities? | YES | NO |

(d) Does the other parent have access or custody? | ACCESS | CUSTODY | NEITHER |

The following section must not be completed by the applicant (See Information Notes 12 (f) & 13)

9 IDENTIFICATION CERTIFICATE (Not to be signed by a relative)   (PLEASE PRINT CLEARLY)

I, ... of ....
(full name)   (residential address)

am over 18 years of age and declare that I have known ....
(full name of applicant)
personally for at least 12 months. **I have also certified on the back of one of the photographs that it is a true likeness of the applicant, whom I have named on the photograph.** To the best of my knowledge and belief the statements made in this application are correct. I have read and understood the warning overleaf.

Telephone numbers: Home: .... Business: ....

SIGNATURE OF CERTIFIER: .... Date: ....

---

10 SIGNATURE   (See Information Note 14)
I have enclosed:
☐ Fee (cheque/postal note/money order/cash $ ....
☐ Birth certificate(s) *(State how many enclosed)*: ....
☐ Two passport photographs, one of which is correctly certified.
☐ Previous passports *(State how many enclosed)*: ....
☐ Other documents *(Please state)*: ....

The information given in this application is true. I have read and understood the warning overleaf.
SIGNATURE OF APPLICANT: ....
Date: ....

---

11 EMERGENCY ADDRESS   (See Information Note 15)

Should an emergency arise during my trip, you may contact my next of kin or close relative in my usual country of residence:

Name: ....
Address: ....
Phone No. ....
Relationship (if any) ....

July 1984

THE WRITTEN DRIVING TEST

INFORMATION TO HELP YOU IN YOUR DRIVING TEST.

Written driving test for a New Zealand driver's license.

**Ministry of Transport
Road Transport Division**

TIPS FOR MOTOR CYCLISTS

1. Study the Road Code and know and understand the rules.
This is an essential prerequisite for all road users.

2. Concentrate all the time
Concentration is the keystone of all good driving; it enables you to see and take notice of every detail, and thus avoid potential accidents. It also ensures skilful handling of your motorcycle. By concentrating, you can prevent bad gear changes and late and fierce braking, and so do away with involuntary skids.

3. Think before acting
A good driver does not ride automatically. Every riding operation is a problem which can only be solved by thinking. Carry out manoeuvres in plenty of time so that you are able to accelerate away from danger or stop to avoid it.

4. Exercise restraint and don't follow too closely
Follow at a safe distance any vehicle which you eventually intend to overtake. You may overtake when you see that the road ahead is clear. "Tailgating" is always a dangerous exercise and you should follow the "two-second" rule presented in Defensive Driving Courses. Using some fixed object (e.g. a lamp post or a road sign), count the time lapse from when the vehicle in front of you passes this marker to when you pass the marker yourself. If the time taken is less than two seconds (counting one thousand and one, one thousand and two), you're following too close for the speed at which you're travelling and you should slow down to increase the distance immediately.

This calls for great restraint, especially when riding a fast motor cycle, but you should never try to overtake or carry out any other manoeuvres unless it can be done with complete safety. Overtaking must always be accomplished in the minimum of time.

5. Use speed intelligently and ride fast only in the right places
It is not always safe to ride at the maximum speed permitted. In some circumstances such a speed is definitely dangerous. Where conditions permit it is best to ride at an even speed as it assists in keeping traffic moving in an orderly and constant stream.

High speeds are safe only when a clear view of the road ahead is possible for a considerable distance. The speed in all cases must be governed by the amount of road that can be seen to be clear, and, of course, by the posted speed limit.

Remember that at 80 km/h a motor cycle travels a distance of about 22 metres in one second. With many riders a second elapses between first seeing an emergency and applying the brakes.

Concentration and alertness are, therefore, absolutely imperative.

6. Develop your motor cycle sense and reduce wear and tear to a minimum
Motor cycle sense is the ability to get the best out of your machine with an entire absence of jerks and vibration. It requires smooth and thoughtful operation of the controls with hands and feet.

This can only be achieved if the operations are carried out in plenty of time. Motor cycle sense adds to your safety factor as you will always be in the right gear at the right time.

7. Be sure your motor cycle is roadworthy and know its capabilities
A defective motor cycle must never be taken out. To prevent this, check your vehicle.

Before attempting to ride a new motor cycle, get accustomed to its controls, acceleration, braking capabilities and characteristics.

8. Perfect your roadcraft and acknowledge courtesies extended to you by other road users
Roadcraft includes every phase of riding. It is something more than road sense. Many people possess the latter but do not make the best use of it owing to lack of control, inability to use the road and position their machine to the best advantage. A rider with good roadcraft knows how to avoid awkward and possibly dangerous situations. Good roadcraft not only prevents accidents, but makes riding less arduous.

9. Wear Protective Clothing
Even if you follow all the advice we've given you here, you can still be involved in an accident. Remember that car drivers tend to look for other cars and often miss seeing motor cyclists. Make yourself as conspicuous as possible. Keep your headlight on dip during the day and wear brightly coloured protective clothing. Remember that approved safety helmets are required by law for all motor cyclists and pillion riders at all speeds. Sensible riders also wear heavy shoes or boots and leather gloves, as toes and fingers can be very vulnerable in an accident. This is just as important in summer, when you may be tempted to wear sandals and light clothing.

The Practical Driving Test

Most test failures result from inadequate or insufficient training. The well trained pupil has no reason to worry about having to undergo the practical driving test and therefore it is wise not to rush your application.

The testing officer is trained to observe accident promoting faults in driving technique and is required to mark demerits accordingly. He is, however, giving a test, not a driving lesson. His job is to find out how well the applicant can drive and he will not overlook errors and omissions even though he may be impressed by the driver's character, attitudes, and potential driving ability. If a failure results, he will make the reasons clear to you at the conclusion of the test and you can be assured that there is nothing personal in his decision.

Applying For The Test

Birth Certificate: All new applicants for licences must produce a birth certificate with their applications.

Where: You should apply to sit the test at the Ministry of Transport's office or local authority's driver testing office in the area where you live.

Vehicle: You must provide a vehicle of the same class as the type for which you want a licence.

Licence Fees: A provisional licence to drive a motor cycle costs $2.00.
A driver's licence for 1 year costs $2.50.
A driver's licence for 2 years costs $5.00
A driver's licence for 3 years costs $7.50
A driver's licence for 4 years costs $10.00
A driver's licence for 5 years costs $12.50

Important: If you already hold a current driver's licence, you must show it to the testing officer. When you make the appointment for your practical test, you must indicate the class of vehicle for which you wish to be tested.

Please report for the test on time: If you are late, in most instances you will have to forego your appointment and make another, as others are booked in immediately following your test.

Driver Test Questionnaire

FORM 1

For each of the questions listed below put a stroke in the square opposite the correct answer.

NOTE—Only one of the answers given is correct.

1. WHAT IS THE MEANING OF THIS SIGN?

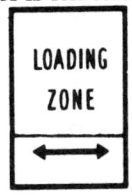

   LOADING ZONE ⟷

   A. Any vehicle may stop to pick up or set down goods or passengers provided the vehicle is not left unattended for more than 5 minutes
   B. Any vehicle except a motor cycle or car may stop to pick up or set down goods provided the vehicle is not left unattended for more than 5 minutes
   C. Only trucks may stop to pick up or set down goods for a maximum period of 5 minutes
   D. Only buses and taxis may stop

2. FROM WHAT POSITION ON AN UNLANED ROAD SHOULD YOU MAKE A LEFT-HAND TURN AT AN INTERSECTION?
   A. The most convenient position to you
   B. No particular place
   C. As close as practicable to the left of the road
   D. As close to the centre line as possible

3. WHAT SHOULD YOU DO WHEN PARKING PARALLEL TO THE KERB ON A STEEP DOWN-GRADE?
   A. Leave the front wheels straight ahead
   B. Turn the front wheels towards the kerb
   C. Turn the front wheels away from the kerb
   D. Run the front and rear left wheels hard against the kerb

4. IF YOU INJURE SOMEBODY IN AN ACCIDENT, WITHIN WHAT PERIOD MUST YOU REPORT IT TO THE NEAREST POLICE STATION, MINISTRY OF TRANSPORT OFFICE, CONSTABLE, OR TRAFFIC OFFICER UNLESS YOU ARE UNABLE TO DO SO BECAUSE OF YOUR INJURIES?
   A. As soon as reasonably practicable, but at least within 2 hours
   B. As soon as reasonably practicable, but at least within 6 hours
   C. As soon as reasonably practicable, but at least within 1 week
   D. As soon as reasonably practicable, but at least within 24 hours

5. WHAT MUST YOU DO WHEN YOU INTEND TO TURN RIGHT FROM A ROAD INTO A DRIVEWAY OR INTERSECTION?
   A. You should signal immediately before you turn
   B. Do not signal unless traffic is approaching you
   C. No signal is necessary
   D. Give a right turn signal at least 3 seconds before you intend to turn

6. HOW IS IT ADVISABLE TO WEAR A LAP AND DIAGONAL SEAT BELT?
   A. With no slack at all between your chest and the seat belt
   B. With about 3 cm slack between your chest and the seat belt
   C. With about 10 cm slack between your chest and the seat belt
   D. As loosely as you like as long as it is comfortable

7. WHAT SHOULD YOU DO IF YOU ARE DRIVING AT NIGHT AND BECOME SLEEPY?
   A. Drive on the shoulder of the road
   B. Pull off the roadway and have a rest
   C. Increase speed so you can get home quickly
   D. Keep on driving but use a lower gear

8. WHAT IS THE SPEED LIMIT AFTER YOU PASS A SIGN ADVISING OF AN ACCIDENT AND UNTIL YOU CLEAR THE ACCIDENT SCENE?
   A. 20 km/h
   B. 30 km/h
   C. 40 km/h
   D. 50 km/h

9. WHAT SHOULD YOU DO WHEN YOU ENCOUNTER STOCK?
   A. Slow right down and pull over to the side of the road
   B. Give a continuous blast on the horn
   C. Give a series of toots on the horn
   D. Race your engine intermittently

10. WHAT IS THE AMOUNT OF ALCOHOL PER 100 MILLILITRES OF BLOOD THAT MUST NOT BE EXCEEDED IF A PERSON IS DRIVING OR ATTEMPTING TO DRIVE A MOTOR VEHICLE ON A ROAD?
    A. 50 milligrams
    B. 100 milligrams
    C. 80 milligrams
    D. 120 milligrams

11. WHAT MUST YOU DO WHEN RED LIGHTS ARE FLASHING AT A RAILWAY CROSSING?
    A. Cross immediately the train has passed
    B. Change into low gear and then cross the line
    C. Stop until the lights cease flashing
    D. Stop and if no train is in sight you may cross

12. ARE YOU PERMITTED TO DRIVE A VEHICLE WITH AN INSECURE LOAD?
    A. Yes—if you drive at less than 20 km/h
    B. Yes—if you display a white flag on the right front corner
    C. Yes—if you have a special licence
    D. No—not under any circumstances

13. MAY YOU PASS A VEHICLE THAT HAS STOPPED OR SLOWED DOWN TO GIVE WAY TO PEDESTRIANS USING A PEDESTRIAN CROSSING?
    A. Yes—in any circumstances
    B. Yes—but only if you slow to less than 10 km/h
    C. No—not under any circumstances
    D. Yes—but only if you stop first and do not have to give way to pedestrians

14. **WHAT SHOULD YOU DO WHEN APPROACHING AN INTERSECTION IF THE TRAFFIC LIGHTS CHANGE FROM GREEN TO AMBER?**
    A. Stop if you can do so safely before entering the intersection
    B. Speed up to reach the intersection before the light changes to red
    C. Stop even if you must stop in the intersection
    D. Swing hard to the left and stop immediately around the corner

15. **HOW OFTEN MUST A WARRANT OF FITNESS BE RENEWED?**
    A. Every 3 months
    B. Every 6 months
    C. Every year
    D. Every 6 weeks

16. **WHEN MUST YOU ALWAYS DIP YOUR LIGHTS?**
    A. In a tunnel
    B. In a limited speed zone
    C. When they might dazzle another driver
    D. Approaching a railway crossing

17. **MUST YOU ALWAYS SIGNAL WHEN TURNING LEFT?**
    A. Yes
    B. No—only when there are vehicles behind you
    C. No
    D. No—only when there are oncoming vehicles

18. **WHEN IS "A" ALLOWED TO PASS "B"?**
    A. In any circumstances but only if it is safe
    B. In any circumstances
    C. Only if B has stopped
    D. Not under any circumstances

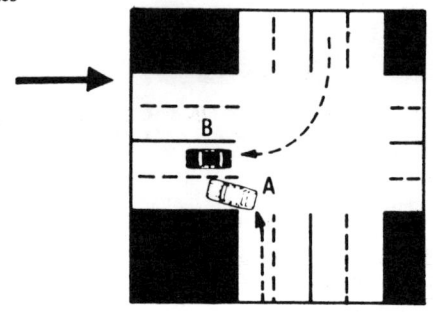

19. **IF YOU ARE FORCED TO TRAVEL AT A SLOW SPEED WHICH MAY HOLD UP OTHER TRAFFIC, WHAT SHOULD YOU DO?**
    A. Travel just to the left of the road centre
    B. Move your vehicle as far as practicable to the left side of the road
    C. Insist that following traffic slows to your speed
    D. If the road is unlaned you should travel down the middle of the road so that vehicle from behind may overtake on the left

20. **WHAT MUST YOU DO WHEN YOU SEE THIS SIGN?**
    A. Slow down to 10 km/h and then proceed only if the way is clear
    B. Stop where you can see whether the way is clear; proceed only if it is
    C. Stop only if you are turning and then proceed if the way is clear

21. **WHAT IS THE MEANING OF THIS MARKING ON THE ROAD?**
    A. There is a pedestrian crossing ahead
    B. There is a school ahead
    C. There are traffic lights ahead

22. **WHAT IS THE CLOSEST DISTANCE YOU MAY FOLLOW BEHIND ANOTHER VEHICLE AT 70 KM/H?**
    A. 20 metres
    B. 24 metres
    C. 28 metres

23, 24, & 25. IN EACH OF THE SITUATIONS SHOWN WHO GIVES WAY?

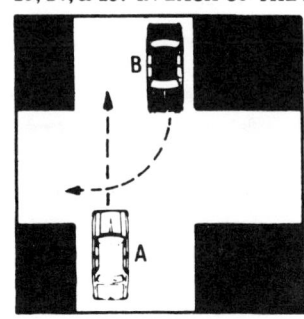

23. A. A
    B. B
    C. Neither

24. A. A
    B. B
    C. Neither

25. A. A
    B. B
    C. Neither

ANSWERS

1	A	6	B	11	C	16	C	21	A
2	C	7	B	12	D	17	A	22	C
3	B	8	A	13	C	18	A	23	B
4	D	9	A	14	A	19	B	24	A
5	D	10	C	15	B	20	B	25	A

Driver Test Questionnaire

FORM 2

For each of the questions listed below put a stroke in the square opposite the correct answer.

NOTE—Only one of the answers given is correct.

1. WHAT MUST YOU DO WHEN YOU SEE TWO RED TRAFFIC LIGHTS FLASHING ALTERNATELY AT THE SIDE OF THE ROAD?
   - A. Slow down and proceed with caution if the way is clear
   - B. Slow down and stop if any other vehicle is coming
   - C. Slow down to 20 km/h
   - D. Stop until the lights cease flashing

2. WHAT IS THE CLOSEST DISTANCE YOU MAY FOLLOW BEHIND ANOTHER VEHICLE AT 50 KM/H?
   - A. 16 metres
   - B. 20 metres
   - C. 24 metres
   - D. 28 metres

3. IF YOU ARE INVOLVED IN AN ACCIDENT WHAT, AS A DRIVER, MUST YOU DO FIRST?
   - A. Report to the nearest Police Station, Ministry of Transport office, constable, or traffic officer
   - B. Drive on if it does not appear that anyone is injured
   - C. Stop and ascertain whether anyone has been injured and render assistance
   - D. Sweep the road clear of broken glass

4. WHICH OF THE FOLLOWING IS TRUE WHEN DRIVING AT NIGHT?
   - A. Sun glasses reduce your night vision
   - B. You car need not have red rear lights so long as a red reflector is showing to the rear
   - C. You must always dip your headlights in a 50 km/h area
   - D. You need not dip your headlights when following another vehicle if you are outside a built up area

5. YOU ARE APPROACHING A CURVE, UNDER WHICH CIRCUMSTANCES MAY YOU PASS ANOTHER VEHICLE?
   - A. If you have 30 m visibility at the start of the movement
   - B. If you have 100 m visibility throughout the whole movement
   - C. If you have 100 m visibility at the start of the movement
   - D. If you have 30 m visibility throughout the whole movement

6. WHERE SHOULD YOU LOOK WHEN MEETING AN APPROACHING CAR AT NIGHT?
   - A. Look at the approaching car
   - B. Look at the centre of the road
   - C. Look at the road to your left of the approaching car
   - D. Look right away from the approaching car

7. MAY YOU PARK A CAR IN FRONT OF A VEHICLE ENTRANCE?
   - A. Yes—provided someone who can move it remains with the vehicle
   - B. Yes—for no longer than 10 minutes
   - C. No—not under any circumstances
   - D. Yes—but only to pick up or let down passengers

8. WHEN MUST YOU ALWAYS DIP YOUR LIGHTS?
   - A. Approaching a pointsman
   - B. Opposite "No Passing" lines
   - C. On a one way street
   - D. Approaching an intersection

9. HOW DO EVEN SMALL QUANTITIES OF ALCOHOL AFFECT YOUR DRIVING?
   - A. By improving your judgment of speed
   - B. By improving your driving ability
   - C. By making you react more slowly
   - D. By making you react more quickly

10. WHAT DOES THIS SIGNAL MEAN?
    - A. I intend to slow down
    - B. I intend to turn left
    - C. I intend to move towards the right
    - D. I intend to stop

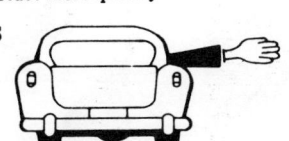

11. WHICH OF THE FOLLOWING IS CORRECT?
    - A. You need never signal when turning or moving left
    - B. You must give at least 6 seconds notice of your intention to turn right unless prevented from doing so by an emergency
    - C. On an uncontrolled pedestrian crossing you must give way to pedestrians on your side of the centre line
    - D. On an unlaned road you may always pass on the left

12. MUST YOU ALWAYS SIGNAL WHEN TURNING LEFT?
    - A. No—only when there are vehicles behind you
    - B. No
    - C. Yes
    - D. No—only when there are oncoming vehicles

13. WHEN MUST YOU SIGNAL IF YOU ARE TURNING TO THE RIGHT UNDER NORMAL CONDITIONS?
    - A. As you are actually turning
    - B. At least 3 seconds before you intend to make your turn
    - C. More than 10 seconds before you intend to make your turn
    - D. Only if there is following traffic

14. FROM WHAT DISTANCE MUST YOUR VEHICLE BE VISIBLE WITHOUT ITS LIGHTS ON IF PARKED AT NIGHT ON AN 80 KM/H SPEED LIMIT ROAD?
    - A. 200 metres
    - B. 100 metres
    - C. 50 metres
    - D. 10 metres

15. **WHAT IS THE FASTEST YOU MAY DRIVE ON A ROAD WITH NO CENTRE LINE?**
    A. At a speed that enables you to stop within the distance of clear road you can see ahead and not faster than the speed limit
    B. At 50 km/h under any circumstances
    C. At a speed that enables you to stop within half the distance of clear road you can see ahead and not faster than the speed limit
    D. At 80 km/h when towing a trailer

16. **WHAT SHOULD YOU DO IN HEAVY TRAFFIC?**
    A. Drive near the centre line
    B. Stop other drivers from taking your space ahead by closing the gap
    C. Keep a space in front and behind relevant to your speed
    D. Move forward when the green light changes to amber for other traffic

17. **YOU MUST NOT MOVE ON TO A RAILWAY LEVEL CROSSING UNLESS –**
    A. You are going fast enough so that you do not stall on the crossing
    B. You have checked that the crossing is not blocked by stationary traffic
    C. You have your headlights on full
    D. You sound your warning device

18. **WHAT IS THE SPEED LIMIT FOR A CAR TOWING A TRAILER?**
    A. 50 km/h
    B. 60 km/h
    C. 70 km/h
    D. 80 km/h

19. **BEFORE MAKING A RIGHT TURN ON A TWO-WAY ROAD YOUR VEHICLE SHOULD NORMALLY BE JUST TO THE LEFT OF THE CENTRE LINE. IF THIS IS NOT SAFE, WHERE ELSE MAY YOU POSITION YOUR VEHICLE?**
    A. As close to the left of the road as practicable
    B. In the middle of the left lane
    C. In the most convenient position for you
    D. Straddling the centre line so traffic from behind you can pass on your left

20. **WHAT DOES THIS SIGN MEAN?**
    A. You may park for 20 minutes between 4 p.m. and 6 p.m.
    B. You may not stop between 4 p.m. and 6 p.m. and may park for only 20 minutes between 8 a.m. and 4 p.m. on days other than Saturdays, Sundays and holidays
    C. You may stop only for a few minutes between 4 p.m. and 6 p.m.

21. **WHAT MUST YOU DO WHEN THIS SIGN IS EXTENDED AT A PEDESTRIAN CROSSING?**
    A. Stop and do not proceed until the sign is withdrawn
    B. Slow down to 20 km/h
    C. Drive on carefully if no children are on your half of the pedestrian crossing

22. **WHEN MAY YOU TRAVEL TO THE RIGHT OF THE BROKEN YELLOW LINE LEADING TO A "NO PASSING" LINE?**
    A. Never
    B. When completing a passing movement
    C. Whenever you like whether you are passing another vehicle or not

23, 24, & 25. **FOR EACH OF THE SITUATION SHOWN, WHO GIVES WAY?**

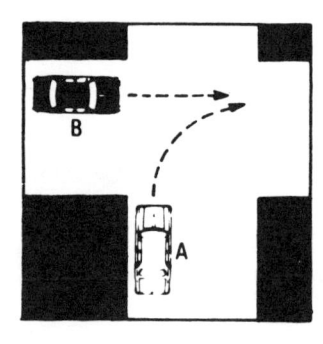

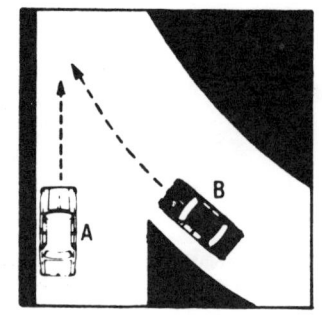

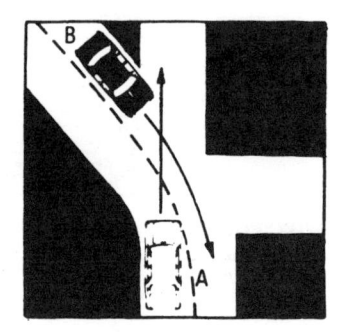

23. A. A
    B. B
    C. Neither

24. A. A
    B. B
    C. Neither

25. A. A
    B. B
    C. Neither

ANSWERS

1	D	6	C	11	C	16	C	21	A
2	B	7	C	12	C	17	B	22	B
3	C	8	A	13	B	18	C	23	A
4	A	9	C	14	B	19	A	24	B
5	B	10	C	15	C	20	B	25	A

Driver Test Questionnaire

FORM 3

For each of the questions listed below put a stroke in the square opposite the correct answer.

NOTE—Only one of the answers given is correct.

1. YOU WISH TO TURN RIGHT FROM A TWO WAY ROAD WITH A CENTRE LINE. WHERE SHOULD YOU POSITION YOUR VEHICLE BEFORE TURNING?
    A. Just to the left of the centre line, or, when it is safer, as far to the left of the road as practicable
    B. To the far left of the road under all circumstances
    C. Straddling the centre line
    D. As far to the right of the centre line as practicable

2. WHAT DOES THIS SIGN MEAN?   **BUS STOP KEEP CLEAR**
    A. You may stop if there are no buses in sight
    B. You may stop between 6 p.m. and 8 a.m. except on Fridays and Saturdays
    C. You may stop provided someone remains in the car
    D. You may not stop at any time

3. WHEN WOULD YOU APPLY THE RULE "GIVE WAY TO YOUR RIGHT"?
    A. At an intersection when yours is the only vehicle controlled by a "GIVE WAY" sign
    B. At an intersection when yours is the only vehicle controlled by a "STOP" sign
    C. At an uncontrolled intersection
    D. When approaching a green traffic signal

4. CAN A DRIVER BE PROSECUTED FOR ALLOWING SOMEBODY ELSE TO RIDE ON HIS VEHICLE IN A POSITION WHICH MIGHT RESULT IN INJURY?
    A. Yes
    B. Only if the person is under 12 years old
    C. Only if the driver is over 21 years old
    D. No

5. WHAT IS THE TOTAL STOPPING DISTANCE SHOWN IN THE ROAD CODE FROM 80 KM/H WITH GOOD BRAKES ON A WET SURFACE?
    A. 149 metres
    B. 101 metres
    C. 66 metres
    D. 41 metres

6. GOOD CAR CONTROL INCLUDES DRIVING –
    A. To the limit of the posted speed restriction
    B. As close as possible to the centre line except where there is oncoming traffic
    C. At the correct speed and in the correct gear and place on the road
    D. With a tight grip on the steering wheel

7. WHEN MUST YOU DIP YOUR HEADLIGHTS?
    A. When approaching a 50 km/h area
    B. In a limited speed zone
    C. In a one-way street
    D. When they might dazzle another driver

8. HOW MUST YOU DRIVE WHEN FOLLOWING ANOTHER VEHICLE?
    A. At such a speed that you can stop in 100 m
    B. So that if the vehicle in front stops suddenly you can stop short of it
    C. Always at the same speed as the vehicle in front and 10 m behind it
    D. Not over 40 km/h

9. WHAT MUST YOU DO WHEN APPROACHING AN INTERSECTION IF THE TRAFFIC LIGHTS CHANGE FROM GREEN TO AMBER?
    A. Speed up to reach the intersection before the light changes to red
    B. Stop if you can do so safely before entering the intersection
    C. Stop even if you must stop in the intersection
    D. Swing hard to the left and stop immediately around the corner

10. MAY YOU PARK A CAR IN FRONT OF A VEHICLE ENTRANCE?
    A. Yes—provided someone who can move it remains with the vehicle
    B. Yes—for no longer than 10 minutes
    C. Yes—but only to pick up or let down passengers
    D. No—not under any circumstances

11. WHAT IS THE BEST WAY TO STOP WHEN DRIVING ON AN ICY OR SLIPPERY ROAD?
    A. Disengage the clutch and brake fairly heavily
    B. Turn off the motor and then apply the brake
    C. Apply the brake very heavily
    D. Pump the brake gently up and down

12. IS THEIR A LAW THAT SAYS YOU MUST MOVE OVER TO THE LEFT OF THE ROAD IF YOU ARE IMPEDING THE NORMAL AND REASONABLE FLOW OF TRAFFIC?
    A. Yes
    B. No—but you should follow this advice
    C. Yes—but only during heavy weekend traffic
    D. No—but you must travel at over 50 km/h on the open road

13. IF YOU ARE DRIVING AT A MODERATE SPEED AND SUDDENLY YOU GET A BLOWOUT IN ONE OF THE TYRES, WHAT SHOULD YOU DO?
    A. Take your foot off the accelerator and try to keep your vehicle on course
    B. Swing your car in the direction it sways towards
    C. Take your foot off the accelerator and brake hard in a straight line
    D. Keep your foot on the accelerator

14. WHAT SHOULD YOU DO IF YOU ARE DAZZLED BY THE LIGHTS OF ANOTHER VEHICLE?
   A. Turn your lights out momentarily
   B. Switch your lights to high beam
   C. Slow down and, if you cannot see, stop
   D. Watch the lights to get a guide as to your position on the road

15. WHAT IS THE SPEED LIMIT FOR MOTOR VEHICLES PASSING A STATIONARY SCHOOL BUS STOPPED TO LET CHILDREN ON OR OFF?
   A. 25 km/h
   B. 20 km/h
   C. 15 km/h
   D. 10 km/h

16. WHAT SHOULD YOU DO WHEN YOU WISH TO TURN RIGHT AT TRAFFIC LIGHTS SHOWING ONLY A GREEN LIGHT AHEAD OF YOU?
   A. Force your way through opposing traffic
   B. Give way to opposing traffic travelling straight ahead
   C. Wait until the lights turn red and then turn quickly
   D. The opposing traffic will give way to you so turn immediately

17. WHAT MUST YOU DO WHEN YOU SEE THIS SIGN? 
   A. Do not exceed 70 km/h if weather conditions, presence of children, density of traffic, etc., would make a higher speed unsafe
   B. Slow down to 70 km/h at night
   C. Do not exceed 50 km/h if weather conditions, presence of children, density of traffic, etc., would make a higher speed unsafe

18. YOU MUST NOT MOVE ON TO A RAILWAY LEVEL CROSSING UNLESS –
   A. You have checked that the crossing is not blocked by stationary traffic
   B. You are going fast enough so that you do not stall on the crossing
   C. You have your headlights on full
   D. You sound your warning device

19. WHEN IS "A" ALLOWED TO PASS "B"?
   A. In any circumstances
   B. In any circumstances but only if it is safe
   C. Only if B has stopped
   D. Not under any circumstances

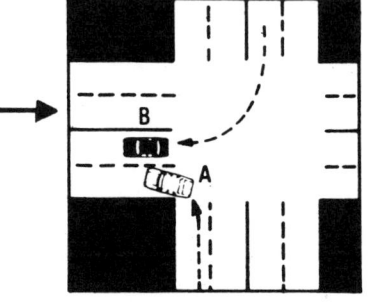

20. WHAT DOES THIS SIGN MEAN?
   A. Do not travel at less than 50 km/h 
   B. Do not exceed 50 km/h unless the road is clear
   C. Do not exceed 50 km/h

21. WHAT DOES THIS SIGN MEAN? 
   A. You may not stop at any time in this length of road
   B. You may stop for 5 minutes between 7 a.m. and 9 a.m. and for any length of time at any other time
   C. You may not stop in this length of road between 7 a.m. and 9 a.m. Monday to Friday except public holidays

22. WHAT DOES THIS SIGN MEAN? 
   A. Change gear – steep hill
   B. Slow down for "S" bend ahead
   C. Slow down for dip in road

23, 24, & 25. FOR EACH OF THE SITUATIONS SHOWN WHO GIVES WAY?

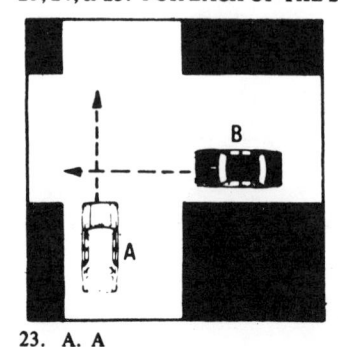

23. A. A
    B. B
    C. Neither

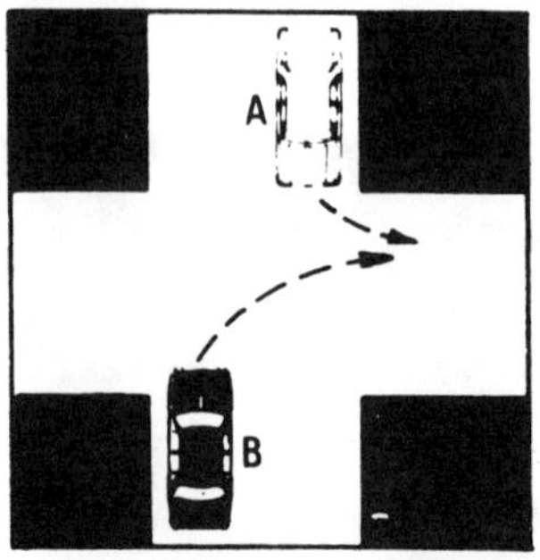

24. A. A
    B. B
    C. Neither

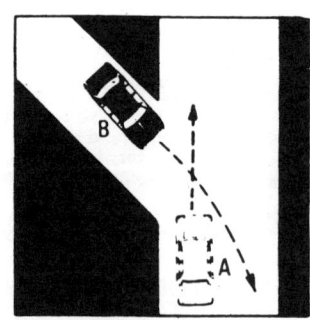

25. A. A
    B. B
    C. Neither

ANSWERS

1	A	6	C	11	D	16	B	21	C
2	D	7	D	12	A	17	C	22	B
3	C	8	D	13	B	18	A	23	A
4	A	9	B	14	C	19	B	24	A
5	B	10	D	15	B	20	C	25	B

Driver Test Questionnaire

FORM 4

For each of the questions listed below put a stroke in the square opposite the correct answer.

NOTE—Only one of the answers given is correct.

1. WHAT DOES THE LAW SAY ABOUT YOUR SPEED WHEN YOU AND ANOTHER VEHICLE ARE APPROACHING AN INTERSECTION?
    A. You may increase speed only if the other vehicle is at least 20 m away from the intersection
    B. Speed up if the other driver has to give way
    C. If your speed is less than the limit you may increase your speed
    D. Do not increase your speed

2. WHAT SHOULD YOU DO IF ANOTHER DRIVER SIGNALS THAT HE IS GOING TO PASS YOU ON A TWO WAY ROAD?
    A. Move to the right so he cannot pass
    B. Speed up so he will not need to pass
    C. Signal him to remain behind you as you feel he is going too fast
    D. Move as far to the left as practicable and do not increase speed

3. IF A GREEN ARROW AND A RED LIGHT SHOW AT THE SAME TIME AT A TRAFFIC SIGNAL, WHICH STATEMENT IS CORRECT?
    A. Providing you give way to pedestrians who are crossing legally, you may proceed in the direction of the arrow
    B. If the arrow points to the right, you may turn right only if there are no vehicles coming from the opposite direction
    C. You must stop until all lights turn green
    D. You may proceed in any direction

4. WHICH OF THE FOLLOWING IS LEGALLY REQUIRED ON ALL MOTOR VEHICLES?
    A. Efficient bumper(s)
    B. Backing light
    C. Rear red reflector(s)
    D. Windscreen washers

5. WHAT IS THE CLOSEST DISTANCE YOU MAY PARK FROM AN INTERSECTION IF NO SPECIAL DISTANCE IS INDICATED BY A SIGN OR ROAD MARKING?
    A. 4 metres
    B. 6 metres
    C. 8 metres
    D. 10 metres

6. AFTER DRIVING THROUGH WATER, WHAT SHOULD YOU DO?
    A. Drive on slowly
    B. Stop the car and apply the hand brake for one minute
    C. Apply the brakes several times to dry out the linings
    D. Refrain from using your brakes for at least 300 m

7. WHEN MAY YOU NOT USE THE WARNING DEVICE ON AN ORDINARY MOTORCAR IN A 50 KM/H AREA (EXCEPT IN AN EMERGENCY)?
    A. Between 4 p.m. and 6 p.m.
    B. Between 2 p.m. and 4 p.m.
    C. Between midnight and 8 a.m.
    D. Between 11 p.m. and 7 a.m.

8. IF THE ONLY WORDS ON A SIGN ARE "NO STOPPING", FOR WHAT PERIOD DOES THE RESTRICTION APPLY?
    A. 9 a.m. – 4 p.m. on any day
    B. 8 a.m. – 6 p.m. on days other than Saturdays, Sundays, or public holidays
    C. 8 a.m. – 6 p.m. on days other than Saturdays, Sundays, or public holidays but until 9 p.m. on Fridays
    D. 9 a.m. – 4 p.m. on weekdays only

9. WHAT IS THE MAXIMUM LEGAL SPEED IN A LIMITED SPEED ZONE WHEN CERTAIN HAZARDOUS CONDITIONS EXIST?
    A. 80 km/h
    B. 70 km/h
    C. 60 km/h
    D. 50 km/h

10. IF YOU ARE TURNING AT TRAFFIC LIGHTS MUST YOU GIVE WAY TO PEDESTRIANS WHO ARE CROSSING LEGALLY WITH THE LIGHTS?
    A. Yes
    B. Not if you are turning in compliance with a green arrow
    C. Only if they are on a pedestrian crossing
    D. Only if they have a "CROSS" light

11. WHAT MUST YOU DO IF GLASS FALLS ON TO THE ROAD FROM YOUR VEHICLE AND YOU ARE ABLE TO REMOVE IT QUICKLY AND SAFELY?
    A. Remove it within 2 hours
    B. Remove it immediately
    C. Remove it within 24 hours
    D. Report it to a traffic officer

12. WHAT MUST YOU DO WHEN FOLLOWING ANOTHER VEHICLE IN WET CONDITIONS?
    A. Keep closer behind it than usual so that you can follow in its tracks
    B. Drive with the hand brake partly on
    C. Keep a greater distance behind than normal
    D. Coast down any hills

13. WHAT SHOULD YOU DO WHEN YOU HEAR A SIREN FROM AN EMERGENCY VEHICLE?
    A. Speed up to get out of the way
    B. Drive up on the footpath to get out of the way
    C. Stop, or make way for the emergency vehicle
    D. Take no special action

14. WHICH ONE OF THE FOLLOWING STATEMENTS IS CORRECT?
    A. Alcohol has no effect on driving ability
    B. Alcohol makes you react more slowly
    C. Alcohol makes you react faster
    D. Alcohol increases your ability to judge speed

15. **WHAT SHOULD YOU DO IF YOUR CAR GOES INTO A SKID?**
    A. Turn the front wheels to keep the nose of the car pointing the way the car is moving
    B. Immediately brake hard
    C. Turn the front wheels away from the direction of the skid
    D. Wait for the skidding to stop

16. **WHICH ONE OF THE FOLLOWING SHOULD YOU USE WHEN DRIVING IN A FOG?**
    A. Sidelights
    B. Upper headlight beams
    C. No lights at all
    D. Dipped headlights

17. **"A" WISHES TO TURN RIGHT. WHICH STATEMENT IS CORRECT?**
    A. A may drive over the white diagonal markings from point X
    B. A may not enter the right lane until point Y is reached
    C. A may only use the right lane if the traffic flow is heavy
    D. A must turn from the left lane

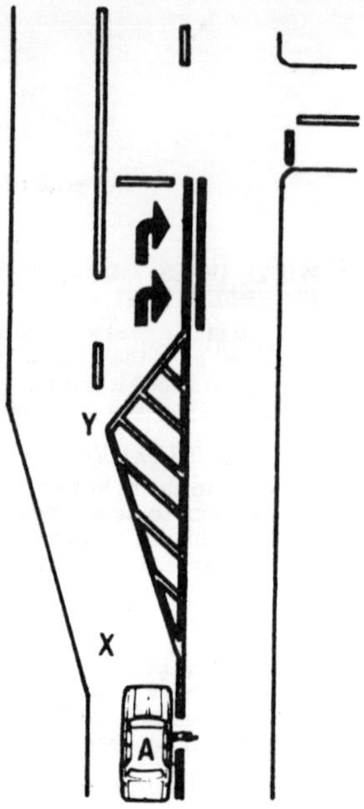

18. **WHAT DOES THIS SIGNAL MEAN?**
    A. I intend to turn right 
    B. I intend to slow down or stop
    C. I intend to reverse
    D. I intend to turn left

19. **WHICH OF THE FOLLOWING IS CORRECT?**
    A. You need never signal when turning or moving left
    B. You must give at least 6 seconds notice of your intention to turn right unless prevented from doing so by an emergency
    C. On an unlaned road you may always pass on the left
    D. On an uncontrolled pedestrian crossing you must give way to pedestrians on your side of the centre line

20. **WHEN PASSING A BUS ON WHICH EITHER OF THESE SIGNS IS MOUNTED**

    SCHOOL BUS   **SCHOOL**

    A. Your speed limit is 20 km/h if the bus has stopped for the purpose of allowing children to get on or off
    B. You should stop and wait for the bus to proceed if it has stopped to allow children to get on or off
    C. Slow down to 10 km/h whether or not children are getting on or off

21. **WHAT DOES THIS SIGN MEAN?**   **ACCIDENT**

    A. There has been an accident. You must not exceed 20 km/h after passing the sign until the road is clear
    B. There have been accidents here in the past — slow down
    C. There has been an accident but the way is now clear

22. **WHAT DOES THIS SIGN MEAN?** 
    A. The 50 km/h applies only to heavy trucks and buses
    B. You should drive round the curve at more than 50 km/h
    C. The advised speed for safe and comfortable driving around the curve is 50 km/h

23, 24, 25. **FOR EACH OF THE SITUATIONS SHOWN, WHO GIVES WAY?**

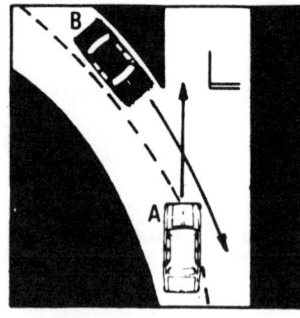

23. A. A
    B. B
    C. Neither

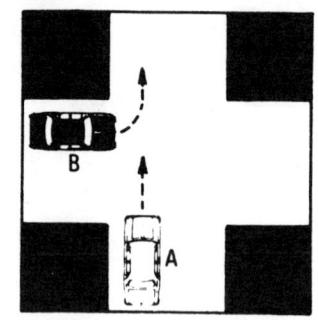

24. A. A
    B. B
    C. Neither

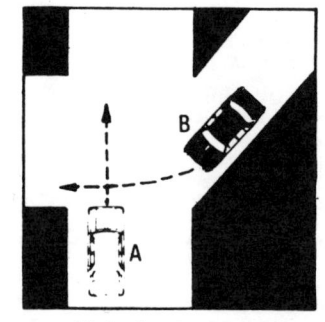

25. A. A
    B. B
    C. Neither

ANSWERS

1	D	6	C	11	B	16	D	21	A
2	D	7	D	12	C	17	A	22	C
3	A	8	B	13	C	18	B	23	A
4	C	9	D	14	B	19	D	24	B
5	B	10	A	15	A	20	A	25	B

Driver Test Questionnaire

FORM 5

For each of the questions listed below put a stroke in the square opposite the correct answer.

NOTE—Only one of the answers given is correct.

1. MAY YOU DRIVE DURING THE HOURS OF DARKNESS WITH ONLY SIDE LIGHTS ON?
   A. Only up to one hour after sunset
   B. Not under any circumstances
   C. Only if street lighting is very good
   D. If you can see substantial objects 30 m away

2. WHAT IS THE SAFEST WAY TO APPROACH ANY INTERSECTION?
   A. By looking steadily to the right
   B. By travelling at the legal speed limit for the locality
   C. By looking steadily to the left
   D. At such a speed that you can stop whether or not you have to give way

3. IF YOUR CAR IS NOT AUTOMATIC (IF IT HAS A HAND-OPERATED GEAR CHANGE) AND IT STALLS ON A RAILWAY CROSSING WHAT IS THE BEST ACTION TO TAKE?
   A. Get out and push the car over the crossing
   B. Wave to attract the attention of the engine driver
   C. Change to low gear and use the starter motor to drive off the line
   D. Turn on the indicators and headlights

4. WHICH OF THE FOLLOWING IS TRUE WHEN DRIVING AT NIGHT?
   A. Sunglasses reduce your night vision
   B. Your car need not have a red rear light so long as a red reflector is showing to the rear
   C. You must always dip your headlights in a 50 km/h area
   D. You need not dip your headlights when following another vehicle if you are outside a built up area

5. YOUR VEHICLE HAS A CURRENT WARRANT OF FITNESS, BUT THE RED REAR LIGHT IS NOT WORKING. CAN YOU BE PROSECUTED FOR THIS?
   A. No
   B. Yes
   C. Only if the warrant is almost due to expire
   D. Only if the light has been out of order for over one week

6. WHERE MUST YOU GENERALLY DRIVE ON A ROAD MARKED IN LANES?
   A. Anywhere provided there is no other traffic about
   B. Just to the left of the centre line
   C. Entirely within the appropriate lane
   D. Not more than 1 m over the edge of the lane

7. WHEN MAY YOU PASS IN A SITUATION WHERE THERE IS A "NO PASSING" LINE AND THERE IS A SINGLE LANE ONLY ON YOUR SIDE OF THE ROAD?
   A. When the continuous line is on your side of the broken line
   B. When both lines are continuous
   C. When you will have at least 100 m visibility throughout the entire time you are over the "no passing" line
   D. When you will have at least 100 m visibility throughout the entire movement and you keep wholly to the left of the "no passing" line

8. WHEN APPROACHING AN INTERSECTION CONTROLLED BY TRAFFIC LIGHTS WHAT MUST YOU DO WHEN A RED LIGHT FACES YOU?
   A. Stop and then proceed carefully
   B. Proceed slowly if no other traffic is approaching
   C. Stop only if other traffic is approaching from your right
   D. Stop and remain stopped until the green light appears

9. WHAT IS THE CLOSEST DISTANCE YOU MAY PARK BEFORE A PEDESTRIAN CROSSING IF NO SPECIAL DISTANCE IS MARKED ON THE ROAD?
   A. 6 metres
   B. 8 metres
   C. 10 metres
   D. 12 metres

10. WHAT DOES THIS SIGNAL MEAN?
    A. I intend to turn right
    B. I intend to reverse
    C. I intend to slow down or stop
    D. I intend to turn left

11. WHERE SHOULD YOUR VEHICLE BE JUST BEFORE MAKING A RIGHT TURN AT AN INTERSECTION?
    A. In the centre of the left lane
    B. As close to the left of the road as possible
    C. To the left of and next to the centre of the road providing it is safe
    D. The most convenient position for you

12. WHICH OF THE FOLLOWING STATEMENTS IS TRUE?
    A. It is always safe to pass a cyclist provided you do not exceed the speed limit
    B. It is always safe to pass a school at 10 km/h less than the speed limit
    C. The speed limit is sometimes too high for the conditions
    D. Provided you do not exceed the speed limit you are driving safely

13. WHEN APPROACHING A STOP SIGN AT AN INTERSECTION WHERE MUST YOU STOP?
    A. 6 m back from the STOP line
    B. No more than 3 metres past the STOP sign
    C. 6 m back from the intersecting roadway
    D. Where you can see if the way is clear but before entering the path of any possible traffic

14. **WHAT IS THE CLOSEST DISTANCE YOU MAY PARK FROM AN INTERSECTION IF NO SPECIAL DISTANCE IS INDICATED BY A SIGN OR ROAD MARKING?**
    A. 6 metres
    B. 4 metres
    C. 8 metres
    D. 10 metres

15. **WHAT IS THE CLOSEST DISTANCE YOU MAY FOLLOW BEHIND ANOTHER VEHICLE AT 70 KM/H?**
    A. 16 metres
    B. 20 metres
    C. 24 metres
    D. 28 metres

16. **WHAT IS THE MEANING OF A YELLOW BROKEN LINE PAINTED ON THE ROAD PARALLEL TO AND ABOUT ONE METRE OUT FROM THE KERB?**
    A. You may not pass
    B. Only heavy vehicles may park here
    C. You may stop for no more than 5 minutes
    D. No vehicle may stop there

17. **IF YOU WANTED TO STOP ON THE ROAD TO WHICH THE ARROW IS POINTING, WHAT WOULD THIS SIGN MEAN?** 
    (NO STOPPING ←)
    A. You may stop for 5 minutes at any time
    B. You may not stop between 8 a.m. and 6 p.m. on days other than Saturdays and holidays
    C. You may not stop at any time
    D. You may stop if someone remains in the car

18. **"Y" WOULD LIKE TO PASS "Z". "Y" WOULD HAVE 100 METRES VISIBILITY THROUGHOUT THE MOVEMENT. WHAT DO THE "NO PASSING" LINES AND ADVANCE WARNING LINES ALLOW?**
    A. Y may pass Z under any circumstances
    B. Y may travel on the right of the solid "No passing" line only if completing a passing movement which was started before A
    C. Y may pass Z between A and B if Y does not cross over the solid "no passing" lines to do so
    D. Y may not pass Z under any circumstances

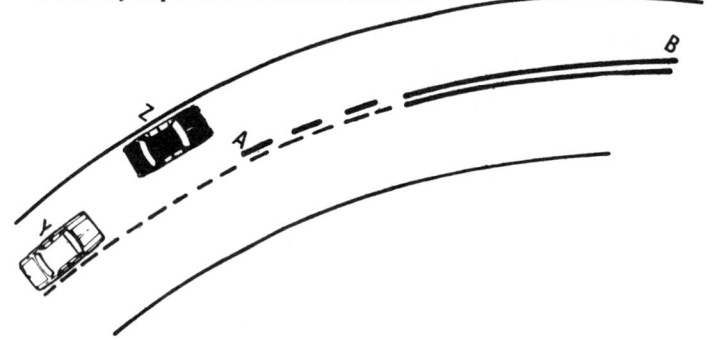

19. **WHAT MUST YOU DO WHEN THIS SIGN IS EXTENDED AT A PEDESTRIAN CROSSING?** 
    (SCHOOL PATROL STOP)
    A. Drive on carefully if no children are on your half of the pedestrian crossing
    B. Slow down to 20 km/h
    C. Stop and do not proceed until the sign is withdrawn

20. **WHAT MUST YOU DO WHEN RED LIGHTS ARE FLASHING AT A RAILWAY CROSSING?**
    A. Cross immediately the train has passed
    B. Change into low gear and then cross the line
    C. Stop until the lights cease flashing
    D. Stop and if no train is in sight you may cross

21. **WHAT MUST YOU DO WHEN YOU SEE THIS SIGN?** 
    (LSZ)
    A. Do not exceed 70 km/h if weather conditions, presence of children, density of traffic, etc., would make a higher speed unsafe
    B. Slow down to 70 km/h at night
    C. Do not exceed 50 km/h if weather conditions, presence of children, density of traffic, etc., would make a higher speed unsafe

22. **WHAT DECIDES THE DISTANCE A CAR TAKES TO STOP ONCE THE BRAKES ARE APPLIED?**
    A. The speed of the car and the condition of the tyres, brakes, and road surface
    B. The visibility distance the driver has
    C. Whether or not the driver has good eyesight

23, 24, & 25. FOR EACH OF THE SITUATIONS SHOWN, WHO GIVES WAY?

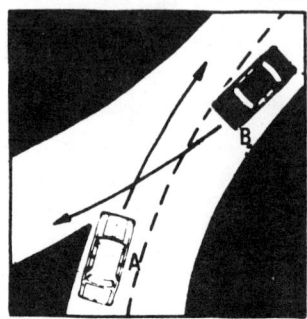

23.
    A. A
    B. B
    C. Neither

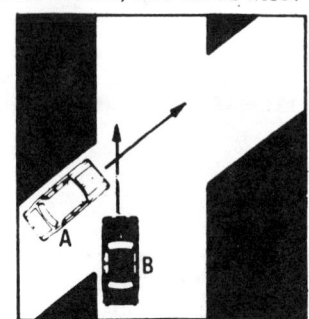

24.
    A. A
    B. B
    C. Neither

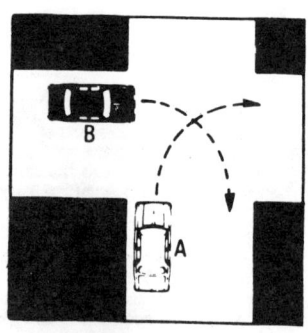

25.
    A. A
    B. B
    C. Neither

ANSWERS

1	B	6	C	11	C	16	D	21	C
2	D	7	D	12	C	17	B	22	A
3	C	8	D	13	D	18	C	23	B
4	A	9	A	14	A	19	C	24	A
5	B	10	C	15	D	20	C	25	B

BE A DEFENSIVE DRIVER

You have studied the Road Code and the questions and answers in this booklet, and have prepared yourself for the tests you must pass before you may have a driver's licence. Remember that having this licence is a privilege, not a civil right. You must exercise this privilege carefully and with consideration. Traffic laws are based on commonsense, but the driver who keeps strictly to them is not immune from accidents caused by a driver who ignores them. A good, responsible driver drives so that accidents are prevented in spite of the incorrect actions of others or of adverse driving conditions. He obeys the law **and** exercises knowledge, alertness, foresight, judgment and skill, and this combination makes him **a defensive driver.**

Defensive Driving Course: This was developed by the National Safety Council of America as a result of research into the proven accident avoidance training programmes conducted by trucking companies for their drivers. It is being made available to all New Zealand drivers by the New Zealand Defensive Driving Council Inc.

Aim: To change the attitudes of drivers if necessary, so that preventable traffic accidents are reduced to a minimum.

What is a preventable accident?: A preventable accident is one in which the driver failed to do everything he reasonably could have done to prevent it. Remember—many collisions are preventable because most traffic situations are predictable.

What does the Defensive Driving Course teach you?: The following is a summary—

1. That the avoidance of accidents is the key to good driving.
2. That accidents are either preventable or non-preventable.
3. That you can learn about the preventability of accidents by studying accident reports.
4. The standard accident prevention formula.
5. How to apply the accident prevention formula to the six positions of the two-car crash.
6. The six adverse driving conditions that can be present when you drive.
7. How to make a pre-trip mental inventory of the adverse conditions before commencing any trip.
8. What is meant by following distance, reaction distance, braking distance, stopping distance.
9. The four basic seeing habits and how to apply them in recognising the hazards when driving.
10. The five elements of defensive driving—knowledge, alertness, foresight, judgment, and skill.
11. Why approaching drivers cross the centre line and what avoidance action can be taken.
12. How to drive around curves allowing for centrifugal force.
13. The four point plan for intersection safety.
14. How to pass and be passed safely.
15. Why one-car accidents occur and how this type of accident can be avoided.
16. How to avoid collisions with other types of vehicles and people and objects.
17. How to drive on motorways.

Applying what the course teaches you: The most common type of motor vehicle accident is the two-car crash. The defensive driver learns how to apply the standard accident prevention formula to the six positions of the two-car crash—from behind, from ahead, from vehicles approaching him, while overtaking, while being overtaken, and at an intersection. Here are some examples:

Rear End Collision: The defensive driver keeps a safe distance behind the vehicle in front by obeying a "2 second rule". He does this by watching the vehicle ahead pass some definite point in the highway, such as a road marking, a lampost, bridge, pillar or signpost. Then he counts to himself "one thousand and one, one thousand and two". That's 2 seconds. If he passes the spot before he finishes those 8 words he is following too close. This rule holds true for any speed.

Reaction time: The defensive driver takes into account the time it will take him to respond to a situation—i.e. about three-quarters of a second if he is 100% alert.

How to corner: Centrifugal force tends to thrust vehicles towards the outer perimeter of a curve, so that the car moving around the inside of the curve can be forced across the road into the path of oncoming traffic, and vehicles moving too fast around the outer perimeter can be trust off the road. To maintain control over his car the experienced driver slows down before entering the curve and accelerates... after leaving it.

At the cross-roads: The Defensive Driving Course teaches a four point plan for intersection safety. The volume of traffic crossing intersections from various angles often confuses drivers and encourages them to do unexpected things. The defensive driver knows he cannot rely on other cars giving way to him, and that confusion, impatience and indecision may cause an accident. The good driver always makes sure he is safe before proceeding through an intersection; he plans his moves in advance and carries them out promptly.

Being passed: This is a normal part of motoring. When being overtaken the good, defensive driver does not increase his speed, but does everything possible to allow the overtaking vehicle to pass safely.

Passing other vehicles: Before overtaking, a good driver keeps his distance, checks to see that the way ahead is clear and that no one is trying to overtake him, signals his intention well in advance, moves out safely, and accelerates, makes sure the motorist he is overtaking has seen him and if necessary taps his horn, signals left then moves back into line. The defensive driver takes a number of points into consideration in this operation. These are some of the things the Defensive Driving Course teaches you. A good defensive driver knows that the avoidance of accidents is the key to good driving and he uses his knowledge to drive without ever having a preventable accident.

Defensive Driving is concerned with Preventability not Blame.

NZ Defensive Driving Councils

Once you get your licence, if you're interested in attending a Defensive Driving Course contact your nearest area council.

CANTERBURY
P.O. Box 1576,
Christchurch. Tel. 792-577

CENTRAL NORTH ISLAND
P.O. Box 264,
Hamilton. Tel. 395-619

HAWKES BAY-GISBORNE
P.O. Box 387,
Napier. Tel. 438-199

NELSON-MARLBOROUGH
P.O. Box 255,
Nelson. Tel. 88-674

NORTHERN
P.O. Box 9431, Newmarket,
Auckland. Tel. 540-248

OTAGO
P.O. Box 5496,
Dunedin. Tel. 45-171

SOUTHLAND
P.O. Box 61,
Invercargill. Tel. 66-435

WELLINGTON
P.O. Box 27-117,
Wellington. Tel. 720-799

WEST COAST, NORTH ISLAND
P.O. Box 4025,
New Plymouth. Tel. 35-385

WEST COAST, SOUTH ISLAND
180 Preston Road, Greymouth.
Tel. Greymouth 6099

EFFECTS OF ALCOHOL AND DRUGS

* You must not drive or attempt to drive with a breath alcohol concentration of more than 500 micrograms of alcohol per litre of breath (500µ g/1).
* You must not drive or attempt to drive with a blood alcohol concentration of more than 80 milligrams of alcohol per 100 millilitres of blood (80mg/100ml).
* You must not drive or attempt to drive under the influence of drink or drugs to such an extent as to be incapable of having proper control of your vehicle.

Most drivers do not understand fully the effects of alcohol. Attention begins to wander at much lower levels than those needed to produce the traditional signs of "drunkenness", such as staggering, slurred speech etc. This is why a person who is not obviously drunk may still be in a dangerous state for driving.

It is entirely your responsibility to decide how much risk of accident or prosecution you are willing to accept or more importantly what risks you will impose on other people. But you should keep the following in mind:
1. A driver who reaches the breath-alcohol or blood-alcohol limits is much more likely to cause an accident than one who is completely sober.
2. Most people know well in advance when they are going to be drinking, so there's plenty of time to arrange to leave your car at home and use alternative transport, or arrange to travel with a non-drinking driver.
3. If you do consider driving after drinking, remember that alcohol is most dangerous
    (a) When you have enough to feel the effects
    (b) When you are tired
    (c) When it is consumed rapidly
    (d) When taken on an empty stomach

You should check with your doctor that prescribed medicines will not affect your driving. Patent medicines usually contain such information on the label. Any medicine that can affect driving is likely to be more dangerous when taken in combination with alcohol, even in small quantity.

cost. One ticket allows use of rail, road, and rail ferry services for fourteen days. Extra days may be purchased after two weeks if required. Contact your local New Zealand tourist office for details and current prices or write to New Zealand Railways, Private Bag, Wellington, New Zealand. The pass/identity card is useful identification, but remember having one will identify you as a tourist.

4. CANADA

Some of the sources I contacted while conducting research for this book indicated that cross-referencing birth and death certificates was par for the course in Canada; therefore, obtaining a birth certificate using the "ghost" method was not possible. More detailed inquiries, however, seem to show that this is not the case at present and, although a cross-referencing system may be adopted in the future, at this time only the birth certificates of babies who died during birth or shortly thereafter are marked "deceased."

Investigators have reason to believe that Josef Mengele—the Nazi war criminal dubbed "The Angel of Death"—entered Canada in 1964 using an assumed name. This discovery will no doubt prompt the Canadian authorities to tighten up the issuance of visa and I.D. documents in general. (Elderly readers of German descent would do well to avoid this particular country—especially if their identification is less than one hundred percent credible!)

BIRTH CERTIFICATE

Should you ask to examine records in a statistics office (for names of birth-certificate candidates), you will have to provide some kind of legitimate-sounding excuse for your request (research of various types, geneology, medical background information). However, if the staff at the office decides your excuse is not good enough, or if their policy is to deter casual examination of records by the public under any circumstances, you will not be able to approach that office again with a different set of excuses. Also keep in mind that although there are no laws which prohibit you from examining the records, the purpose of the exercise may be defeated if you are required to supply a lot of personal information about yourself to the clerk.

Although it is not a cheerful experience, looking around the graveyards will provide plenty of suitable candidates whose identification you could adopt. Look for childern who died young, and who would be closer to your apparent age had they lived. You can, of course, choose older persons for your new identity, but bear in mind that the longer they lived, the more information there will be about them on record.

Where possible, you should try to select a person who died in an area other than that in which he was born. This information will not appear on gravestones but can be ascertained if you research the obituary columns of newspapers, which can be found in most major libraries. Do your own cross-referencing by selecting an identification from the graveyard and then check newspapers from the relevant year and month until you find mention of the death or burial. Even such basic information as the deceased's name, dates of birth and death, and parent's names will be sufficient to enable you to apply for a birth certificate.

The certificates are issued by the vital statistics offices of the individual states. You will be asked the name, date, and place of birth, and parents' names of the person whose certificate you require. If you apply at the office in person, you will be required to complete a form, and, although different offices have different established practices, you may as well count on having to show some identification of your own. You can say you are the person in question and show some supportive identification, or pretend to be a relative or friend. You can even pretend to be conducting research of some sort. If you write to the office—giving as much information as possible about the person whose certificate you require—there is a strong chance that the certificate will be sent to you without your having to complete an applica-

81

tion form. Enclose a cover letter which explains your reasons for wanting the certificate!

The addresses of the statistics offices can be found in any telephone directory; if you make initial inquiries from outside the country, your local main library will find the addresses for you. Some major city libraries have microfilm copies of telephone directories from other countries, making such research so much easier.

SOCIAL INSURANCE NUMBER

There are I.D. requirements for obtaining a Social Insurance card and number in Canada, but once you meet these requirements, getting the card itself is no problem. Apply at a local office of the Canadian Employment Commission—the equivalent of an English Social Security office—and jump into your why-I-haven't-got-a-card routine. You will have to show a birth certificate and other identification. A driver's license would be good; an electric bill would do.

You will have to complete some forms, which are sent to a main office for processing. The card will be sent to you a couple of weeks later.

The success or failure of these applications may be determined by the excuse you use for not already having a Social Insurance number. There are a few good excuses: For example, you can say you have been living in the United States. The old favorite about how you were illiterate or dyslexic and could not bear the humiliation of having to explain your situation at interviews is always worth considering.

Surprisingly enough, Canadian authorities are not overly fussy about the reasons—providing you can prove who you are with a good I.D.—as they would much prefer to have people pigeonholed as soon as possible. Once again, do not make a big deal about asking for assistance. You might like to explain that you have been making a living doing casual jobs, and government assistance is therefore of little interest to you.

MEDICAL CARD

There is no real equivalent in Canada to the English medical card (which guarantees the holder free or heavily subsidized health care and medical treatment). Instead, there exists a comprehensive insurance system operated by the various provincial governments. The "medical card" in this case is more likely to be evidential proof that the individual is registered either with a provincial government or is insured with a private company.

My advice is that if you intend to establish yourself in Canada, full-time so to speak, seek advice from the medical authority in the province where you will be residing. Should you feel obliged to use some excuse for your lack of knowledge (and insurance), explain that you have been living in the United States with friends or relatives for a considerable period of time and are therefore ignorant of local regulations and requirements. If you prefer to keep your options open, register with a recognized medical insurance company before you enter Canada. Doing so will automatically ensure that you have some solid identification and that you will be adequately covered should you require medical assistance. You will also thus minimize the possibility of being asked awkward questions by authorities should you be involved in an accident.

I have a friend who was traveling in Canada under an assumed name and was to collect a passport in a new name from a contact in Canada. Unfortunately, before he could collect the passport, he was involved in an auto wreck and sent off to the local hospital. A search of his belongings did not turn up any identification and the police were notified. They waited until my friend had recovered sufficiently to answer some questions, and explained to him that unless he could satisfy them as to his identity and right to be in the country, all sorts of nasty things would befall him. He couldn't, and they did! *Be warned.*

Blue Cross members can join the "Canada Health Plan for Visitors to Canada" at a very reasonable cost. Applications can be found at drugstores, travel agencies, and hospitals.

Canada does not offer the same sort of welfare benefits as New Zealand or England, but neither is its system as restrictive and punitive as that of the United States.

DRIVER'S LICENSE

Identification is required before you can obtain a Canadian driver's license, and all the offices I contacted stated that a birth certificate and anything else showing the applicant's name and address, or just the name, would suffice. The licenses issued by different provinces are valid for different lengths of time, usually between one and five years. It makes sense to apply for one which does not have to be renewed frequently. Applicants are required to take a written test as well as the driving test. If you are new to the area, take some time to study the road signs and traffic regulations.

Unlike countries operating a centralized issuing system, Canadian licenses are frequently made at the point of the examination and handed over on the spot. The fee is around ten Canadian dollars but varies slightly from province to province. Not all Canadian licenses carry a photo of the holder, but it is safe to assume that those that do have more weight in the eyes of police officials than those that do not.

Apparently, there have been quite a few people prosecuted in Canada for trying to obtain (or actually obtaining) a license under an assumed name, many of whom had had their own licenses revoked. However, there are plenty of people who never learn to drive until later in life, so regardless of your age, if the clerk at the examination center seems suspicious, don't worry. One of the most common ways to deter would-be frauds is to make the simplest interview seem like the third degree.

PASSPORT

The procedure for obtaining a passport in Canada is very similar to that which exists in England. The application form can be obtained from a post office, travel agent, or passport office. Three photographs of the applicant must be submitted, and they must not be larger than 2" by 2¾" with a space for a signature at the bottom. The photographer has to declare where and when he took the pictures, and he must sign to the effect that they are actually pictures of the applicant.

As with the English application, a guarantor must sign a declaration stating that he has known the applicant for at least two years, and he must be a doctor, lawyer, policeman, or other professional. However, if the applicant does not know anyone who can act as guarantor for him, he may complete Form PPT 132, which is a declaration in lieu of a guarantor. This form *must* be competed in the presence of, and witnessed by, a commissioner of oaths or a notary public. This form allows the applicant to explain why he or she cannot provide a guarantor and contains a lot of personal questions.

Once the application forms are completed, they should be sent to the passport processing center in Ottawa, along with a birth certificate, fee payment, signed photographs, and Form PPT 132 (if applicable). The passport and birth certificate will be sent back to you within a few weeks, depending on the volume of applications being received by the processing office at the time.

As with most of the government-issued application forms, passport applications are self-explanatory, but *always* read them through a few times before you start to fill out the form. If your birth certificate is good and solid, you will have no problems at all in securing a Canadian passport. The authorities are keen to spot known criminals trying for a fresh start, but the sheer numbers of applications received means that there is little time and funding left over for investigating everyone about whom they have doubts.

5. GENERAL TECHNIQUES AND INFORMATION

DECODING GOVERNMENT PIN AND REFERENCE NUMBERS

To decode such numbers, you need *at least* two examples of the documents bearing the coded information, as well as the precise details of how, when, where, and to whom they were issued. These requirements are easily achieved by enlisting the aid of two individuals to whom similar documents have been issued.

It is now a simple matter of comparing the documents with the actual information provided by the holders. In so doing, you can determine what each symbol represents. The example below shows how to determine possible links between the code and the details it conceals. Most of the code systems used are logical and fairly easy to decipher. They are used often by authorities as a type of shorthand rather than as a serious attempt to prevent other people from understanding them. Such codes also deter small-time counterfeiters who would not bother to accurately decode the number and letter sequences.

The coded information shown on two identity cards is shown below, and the actual information supplied by the holder is indicated below each code. By comparing the code and the information below it and using the process of elimination, you can decipher the meaning of each symbol.

SMITH.L.F.7.1.50.4.4.M.33.

Name: Fredrick Loyd Smith.
DOB: 4/4/50.
Number of cards issued 1.
Month of issue July.

BROWN.A.J.3.2.41.11.9.F.57.

Name: Jane Anne Brown.
DOB: 9/11/41
Number of cards issued 2.
Month of issue March.

The transposition of the surname and initials is easy to detect and should be the first common denominator you consider. It is also frequently used as a simple code on many European documents.

The date-of-birth reference should be considered next. It is usually easy to decipher but can sometimes be confusing if both the day and month have identical numbers (3/3, 7/7, and so on).

Note: The date abbreviation system used in the United States puts the *month* first, followed by the day. For example, 8/5/85 would translate as the *5th day of the 8th month, '85*. In England and many other countries, however, the same abbreviation translates as the *8th day of the 5th month, '85*.

Having decoded the name and date-of-birth symbols, the next stage is to compare any other known information with symbols appearing on the document. If we look at the third character on the identity cards and check it against the information given by the holder, we can see that it represents the month of issue (in Smith's case, July—the 7th month).

The penultimate character differs on each card, and cross-checking will reveal whether it refers to any specific aspect of the holder's personal details or to details pertaining to the document itself, such as the type, number of previous issues, etc.

In this example shown herein, it is quickly seen that the "M" or "F" characters denote the holder's sex, though the sex symbols will not always be as obvious as they are here. Be sure to check for this thoroughly.

In the example given, the character sequence allocated to the surname of the holder consists of five letters. In the case of names such as Smith, Brown, etc., this is sufficient to allow the full surname to be included on the document. However, if the name were, for example, Turner, the PIN would show only Turner as the surname.

It is worth checking to see how many letters are allocated to the surname—if it is not given in full—by cross-referencing with holders who have both long and short surnames. Other code systems may be similar in design to the "Soundex" system in which groups of similar sounding letters are designated a code number (m and n = 5, d and t = 3, and so on). In the United States, the Soundex system is used on some driver's licenses to form a four-digit code from the first letter of the surname and the following three consonants (doubled consonants are not counted). The consonants w, h, and y are not coded, and neither are the vowels. There are variations in use elsewhere.

Alternate codes may take the form of a simple letter/number designation (a = 1, b = 2, etc.) or a variation thereof. The year of birth may be deducted from, say, 200 or 100, and be shown on the document as that figure (i.e., year of birth is 59 [100 − 59] might be shown as 41). There are hundreds of similar codes in use, but all of them can be deciphered if you have access to the information supplied by the holder at the time the document was issued.

Why local authorities bother with these complicated, joke codes is a mystery to me. I know of at least one, simple, foolproof, and undecipherable code system that could be implemented quickly and would not be expensive to operate. It could be used day or night to confirm or refute the identity claim of anyone carrying a document bearing the code. It could never be counterfeited or illegally transferred. As I said, I know of at least one such system. *You* may well know—or be able to design—several. You can guarantee that "the powers that be" know of hundreds. So, why aren't they used? Think about it!

Forgery and counterfeiting aside, it is useful to know *exactly* what information, in code form, appears on certain documents since such knowledge enables the holder to determine what *additional* (accurate!) information he must give in order to "pass" an I.D. check. (This is especially important if the check is made at such a time as to prevent the inquisitor seeking confirmation from the issuing authority.) For example, upon deciphering a document, it may be found that it shows only the age of the holder but not the precise date of birth, or it may show the name and date of birth but not the address, or it may indicate the height but not the color of the eyes, etc.

SUPPORTIVE IDENTIFICATION

Supportive identification is any document which lends some support to your identity claim, while not necessarily being of sufficient substance to prove you are who you say you are in itself. Few people carry only official documents and no personal items; on occasion, being able to produce *only* a driving license, for example, may arouse more suspicion than if one were to claim "empty pockets."

Supportive identification is usually most effective when "discovered by accident." As an example, imagine the police stop you during a routine check. When asked for your identification, it can be more effective to apparently fumble in your pockets, looking for something with which to prove your identity, and offer a letter (bearing your name and address) and *then* a more solid type of I.D. document, rather than have the solid I.D. ready and waiting (almost as if you *expected* to be asked to prove who you were!).

To this end, the following list of suitable supportive identification will be of use to you. The governments of England, Australia, and New Zealand *do not* issue, or require citizens to carry, any specific form of identification. What an individual considers adequate identification will depend entirely on the circumstances.

Letters: Letters from a close friend or spouse which express good wishes regarding your recent change of address, new job, etc. The more intimate the letter is, the better (within reason of course!). Keep the letter in its envelope—which should clearly show the address and name being used by the holder and a recent postmark.

Photographs: Photos showing the holder with

a spouse or girlfriend are very effective as supportive I.D., especially if used in conjunction with letters.

Rent books or receipts: If you do not have a legitimate rent receipt, blank books and receipts can be bought from large stationery supply outlets in England, Australia, and New Zealand. (There is a branch of W. J. Smith, for example, in most of the major cities, which sells a wide range of related material.) Landlords in these countries will have purchased their rent books or receipt pads from the same (or a similar) place, so there is no forgery involved here.

International Driver's License

Although, as a rule, law-enforcement officials in most countries accept driver's licenses of foreign nationals as identification, it always pays to have that little extra I.D. ready. A good example of this is the IDP—International Driving Permit, which is especially useful if the normal driver's license does not carry a photograph of the holder.

An IDP can be obtained by applying to a local office of any of the motoring organizations. The applicant must be over eighteen years of age and hold a valid normal license (age restrictions may vary from place to place, from time to time). A photograph of the usual passport size will be required. Fees, of course, also vary but are generally minimal.

Vehicle Registration Document

Vehicle registration documents can often be used as effective identification by pedestrians who "have left the car at home for a change." Buying a vehicle is the easiest way of determining exactly what procedures must be complied with in order to obtain the document or to get an existing document transferred into your name. The forms for this are self-explanatory, and carry fee details along with the addresses of the area office to which you should apply.

In England, Australia, New Zealand, and most other countries that issue vehicle registration documents, a central computer is used to store information about the owner and/or driver of the vehicle. Police can access this information from their car via a radio link, enabling them to establish the identity of the registered owner or driver before they stop and question him. Spot checks are often made in this fashion. As long as the driver gives the same information as that which is pulled from the computer, the matter will end there—unless some offense has been committed, of course. In New Zealand, a registration document can be used as identification when dealing with the Social Welfare Department.

As an example of the different degrees of bureaucracy likely to be encountered in English, Australian, and New Zealand government departments, I have included herein samples of the vehicle registration applications for each of those countries. The English application is by far the simplest, relating only to the vehicle registration proper, whereas the Australian and New Zealand documents provide for a transfer of insurance as well (i.e., the cost of the minimum vehicle accident insurance required by law is added to the cost of the road fund or vehicle license). In England, insuring the vehicle is a totally separate process. Similarly, New Zealand laws require that the vehicle be sold with a minimum "warranty of fitness" validity of five months, but Australia and England have no such restrictions. All three systems require notification of sale or transfer to be made by both the seller and the buyer. It is important, therefore, that the buyer not give information on the application form that is different from the information he gave to the seller of the vehicle!

There is no fee for a simple transfer in England, but as can be seen from the Australian form, the fee is eight dollars at the present time and is payable by the new owner. In New Zealand, the *seller* is primarily responsible for paying the fee! It is worth noting that in all three countries, the forms indicate that it is an offense, punishable by a fine, to make false statements and/or to fail to comply with the legal requirements. (Loss of revenue is the real reason for this attitude, although some would say that it prevents drivers who have had accidents from avoiding their responsibilities. Loss of revenue, or the fear of it, is responsible for many of the strange variations in local bureaucracy. This explains why certain documents—important to you and me—may be obtained with the minimum of fuss and form-filling, while other, less "useful" ones can only be obtained after expending large quantities of money, paper, and ink.)

Other Useful Cards

Library card: Obtaining a library card is a matter

Notification of Sale or Transfer

If you sell or transfer the vehicle to someone else, **COMPLETE AND DETACH** this section and send it to DVLC SWANSEA SA99 1AR. **Please do this at once-it is in your own interests to do so.** Give the top part of this document to the new keeper so that he can use it to notify that he has acquired the vehicle.

V5/1 Rev Sept 81

Registration Mark [ ] T 3 03 4

Name and Address of new Keeper or dealer acquiring vehicle

Mr 1 Mrs 2 Miss 3 *Please tick box or give other title below*

Date of Sale or Transfer [ ] 5   Official Use Only 6

Other title e.g. Dr., Rev. or company name

If you have sold or transferred the vehicle to a motor dealer or insurance company, tick here 7

Christian or forenames 8

Surname 9

I sold/transferred this vehicle to the person whose name and address I have written opposite, on the date I have given above. I have also given him/her the top portion of this document.

Address

10

Post Town 11

Signature _____

Postcode

NOTE: The new keeper must also notify the change in Section 1 overleaf; otherwise a new Registration Document will not be issued.

Seller's copy of the English Registration Change Application form.

Notification of Changes

You must notify changes **IMMEDIATELY**. Complete the appropriate section(s) below in **BLACK INK** and **BLOCK LETTERS**, sign the declaration and send the document to DVLC, Swansea SA99 1AR, UNLESS you also require a vehicle licence. In this case the notification must accompany your licence application and be submitted to a licensing post office or Local Vehicle Licensing Office - see licence application form for details.

SECTION 1 - NAME AND ADDRESS OF VEHICLE KEEPER (if different from that printed overleaf).

Mr 1 Mrs 2 Miss 3 *Please tick box or state other title below*   W 4 Official Use Only

(a) If your name is different from that shown overleaf please enter new details opposite

Other title e.g. Dr., Rev. or company name

Christian or forenames 5

Surname 6

(b) If your address is different from that shown overleaf please enter new details opposite

Address

7

Post Town 8

Postcode 9   Day Month Year

(c) If the change is because you are the new keeper please tick this box and give the date you acquired the vehicle. You must also give your name and address in the above boxes if you have not done so already.

K 10   11   C/D 12

The above material is extracted from the buyer's copy of a notification of changes form used in England. Other sections of the same form are used to notify the DVLC of changes in the vehicle's color or engine size. There is no fee for changing the vehicle's registered ownership in England.

IMPORTANT — Please refer to "Information for Owners" on the back before completing this form.
— Please PRINT clearly and firmly using ballpen.

NOTICE OF CHANGE OF OWNERSHIP OF MOTOR VEHICLE M.R.13

Registered under the Transport Act 1962

REGISTRAR'S COPY

To be completed by Registered Owner

I/We

SURNAME (Please print)

CHRISTIAN OR FIRST NAMES IN FULL (Please print)

give notice that the vehicle described has been disposed of to the new owner entered below.
I certify that these particulars given are correct.

SIGNATURE OF REGISTERED OWNER AND DATE OF DISPOSAL

/ /19

If joint ownership, the signature of EACH joint owner is required. In the case of a company, firm or partnership etc., show the capacity of the signatory.

REGISTRATION PLATE No.

MAKE

MODEL (See Note 1b)

YEAR OF MANUFACTURE

ENGINE NUMBER

CHASSIS NUMBER

TYPE (See note 1c)

MOTIVE POWER (See Note 1d)

COLOUR (See Note 1e)

DISTANCE RECORDER READING
KM
MILES
— delete not applicable —

New Owner Details

Title | Surname of Owner (Please print)

Christian or First Names in full (Please Print)

Residential address — A Rural Delivery or Private Box number is not a sufficient address. Name of street or road must be included

Flat house No.
Street or road
Suburb
Town, city or locality
Contact Telephone No.

Postal address — Only required if different from above residential address

OCCUPATION

Vehicle's certificate of registration to be delivered to:

I certify that the particulars given above are correct.

SIGNATURE OF NEW OWNER

If joint ownership the signature of EACH joint owner is required

Date stamp and initials of receiving officer

For Office Use

Evidence of issue of Warrant of Fitness produced and details noted on Certificate of Registration (vehicles over 20 yrs old only)

Certificate endorsed

Certificate forwarded to new Reg. Owner

Certificate forwarded to Authorised Agent (see above)

Tick as necessary to indicate that action taken

REGISTRATION PLATE No.

CERTIFICATE No.

FEE

Checked by ....

DATE STAMP

The actual New Zealand Change of Ownership Application consists of the registrar's copy, the secretary's copy, and an accounting copy.

Motor Registration Division, 60 Wakefield Street, Adelaide, S.A. 5000 (Telephone 227 9911) and Branch Offices

Application for Transfer of Registration

This form is to be completed by the **new owner** of a registered motor vehicle when transferring Registration and Third Party Insurance, and forwarded with $8.00 TRANSFER FEE and the appropriate Stamp Duty (if applicable) to the Registrar of Motor Vehicles within 14 days of the date of purchase or acquisition.

A certificate of registration will be forwarded to the new owner when the transfer has been processed.

PLEASE READ THE INSTRUCTIONS ON THE BACK OF THIS FORM

HEAVY PENALTIES ARE PRESCRIBED FOR FALSE STATEMENTS

Registered Number	I am over the age of sixteen years and hereby apply for the registration of the Vehicle **Registered Number**_____ to be transferred to me.	Date of purchase or acquisition
Name — Full name of proposed Registered owner — See Instruction 1	Please use BLOCK LETTERS ☐ Tick if Business or Company Name 1st Name — Other Names — Last Name (Surname)	
Residential Address — The Address at which the proposed Registered Owner is ordinarily resident — See Instruction 2		Occupation Postcode
Postal Address — See Instruction 3		Postcode
Previous Registered Ownership Name and Address of Person or Firm from whom vehicle purchased/acquired — See Instruction 4		Postcode
Concession — See Instruction 5	Is the vehicle registered at CONCESSION RATES? YES/NO. If YES, state Concession _____ NOTE—If YES, you are required to either: ☐ Pay an additional fee to adjust the registration to UNRESTRICTED USE, or ☐ Lodge with this application the appropriate or similar concession declaration if you are entitled to the same concession. (Please tick appropriate box to indicate the action you intend to take)	
Description of Vehicle	Type — Make — Model — Engine Number (Vehicle or cycle) Chassis/Frame No. — Mass (weight) in kg. (Trailer only) — No. of Wheels (Trailer only) — Registration expires	
Value and Stamp Duty — See Instruction 6	I declare the value of this vehicle/cycle to be ..... $ _____ (Value not required for trailers) Forwarded with this application is the amount of $ _____	Stamp Duty $_____ Transfer Fee $8.00 TOTAL $

Cheques should be made payable to—"MOTOR REGISTRATION DIVISION" and marked "NOT NEGOTIABLE"

SIGNATURE OF APPLICANT _____ Address of applicant (if not new owner) _____

Where a person signs on behalf of the applicant, such person may be held responsible for all statements made. _____

FOR OFFICE USE

Cl.	Registration No.	C.D.	Date of Acquisition		Year	Cubic Capacity if Motor Cycle		Initials	
Trans Type	Seller's Notice	Rebate	Transfer Missing		Common Expiry	Interstate Address	Balance of Fee Calculation— Registration period SIX/TWELVE months	Additional Fee	Assessed
CT 605							General Fee = $ Concession Fee = $ _____ Difference = $ _____ (Difference/1 X No. of Complete months/6 or 12)	Transfer Fee $8.00	
Transfer Missing Details from—								Total TRF	Checked
to—							_____/1 X _____/6 or 12	Stamp Duty SDY	
Comm. Date of Regn.	Expiry Date	Fee Code	Rebate	6 or 12 Mths.	P.M.			Total Fee	

The Australian registration transfer application is self-explanatory, consisting of just one sheet.

INSTRUCTIONS

(1) **Name of Owner**

If a vehicle is owned and to be registered in one person's name or joint names of more than one person, the full name of each owner is to be stated and that person or persons must be over sixteen years of age.

If a vehicle is owned by a corporate body the full name as registered with the Registrar of Companies is to be stated. If the company is not registered in South Australia, a copy of the company registration certificate from the State where the company is registered is to be produced with this application.

If the vehicle is owned and to be registered in a trading name registered under the Business Names Act, the full name as registered is to be shown.

(2) **Address of Owner**

The permanent place of abode (residence) must be shown for persons. Where the vehicle is in joint names of persons living at different addresses, the address of the person having control of the vehicle is to be shown.

Where the vehicle is registered by a corporate body or in a trading name the principal place of business is to be stated.

(3) **Postal Address**

A postal address shown in addition to the above will be used on registration documents **only** where there is no postal delivery to the place of residence of persons or to the place of business of corporate bodies or other organisations or where the postal authorities require a postal address to be used.

(4) **Previous Ownership**

The name of the person or firm from whom the vehicle was purchased or acquired is required. This is not necessarily the last registered owner.

(5) **Concession Registrations**

A registration at concession or reduced rates can be transferred if—
  (a) The new owner is entitled to the same concession and lodges with this application the appropriate concession declaration; or
  (b) The balance of fee for unrestricted use is paid.

(6) **Stamp Duty**

(a) Calculation of stamp duty—all vehicles except Trailers

Value	Stamp Duty all vehicles	Value (continued)	Stamp Duty all Vehicles except Trailers, Tractors owned by Primary Producers and Commercial Vehicles	Stamp Duty all Tractors owned by Primary Producers and Commercial Vehicles	Value (continued)	Stamp Duty all vehicles except Trailers, Tractors owned by Primary Producers and Commercial Vehicles	Stamp Duty all Tractors owned by Primary Producers and Commercial Vehicles
$	$	$	$	$	$	$	$
1- 500	5	3 001-3 100	64	63	5 601-5 700	168	141
501- 600	6	3 101-3 200	68	66	5 701-5 800	172	144
601- 700	7	3 201-3 300	72	69	5 801-5 900	176	147
701- 800	8	3 301-3 400	76	72	5 901-6 000	180	150
801- 900	9	3 401-3 500	80	75	6 001-6 100	184	153
901-1 000	10	3 501-3 600	84	78	6 101-6 200	188	156
1 001-1 100	12	3 601-3 700	88	81	6 201-6 300	192	159
1 101-1 200	14	3 701-3 800	92	84	6 301-6 400	196	162
1 201-1 300	16	3 801-3 900	96	87	6 401-6 500	200	165
1 301-1 400	18	3 901-4 000	100	90	6 501-6 600	204	168
1 401-1 500	20	4 001-4 100	104	93	6 601-6 700	208	171
1 501-1 600	22	4 101-4 200	108	96	6 701-6 800	212	174
1 601-1 700	24	4 201-4 300	112	99	6 801-6 900	216	177
1 701-1 800	26	4 301-4 400	116	102	6 901-7 000	220	180
1 801-1 900	28	4 401-4 500	120	105	7 001-7 100	224	183
1 901-2 000	30	4 501-4 600	124	108	7 101-7 200	228	186
2 001-2 100	33	4 601-4 700	128	111	7 201-7 300	232	189
2 101-2 200	36	4 701-4 800	132	114	7 301-7 400	236	192
2 201-2 300	39	4 801-4 900	136	117	7 401-7 500	240	195
2 301-2 400	42	4 901-5 000	140	120	7 501-7 600	244	198
2 401-2 500	45	5 001-5 100	144	123	7 601-7 700	248	201
2 501-2 600	48	5 101-5 200	148	126	7 701-7 800	252	204
2 601-2 700	51	5 201-5 300	152	129	7 801-7 900	256	207
2 701-2 800	54	5 301-5 400	156	132	7 901-8 000	260	210
2 801-2 900	57	5 401-5 500	160	135	8 001-8 100	264	213
2 901-3 000	60	5 501-5 600	164	138	8 101-8 200	268	216

Where the Value of the Motor Vehicle exceeds $8 200:—

(i) All vehicles except Trailers, Tractors owned by Primary Producers and Commercial Vehicles—

$268 plus $4 for every $100 or fractional part of $100 of the excess over $8 200 of that value.

(ii) Tractors owned by Primary Producers and Commercial Vehicles—

$216 plus $3 for every $100 or fractional part of $100 of the excess over $8 200 of that value.

(b) Exemptions from Stamp Duty

All trailers are exempt. Other available exemptions are described in the form below, which should be completed if applicable.

Licensed dealers and distributors are required to pay stamp duty on all vehicles purchased for use in the business

CLAIM FOR EXEMPTION FROM OR REDUCTION OF STAMP DUTY

I/We Name
of Address

being the applicant/s for transfer of registration of the vehicle described over, hereby claim exemption from or reduction of Stamp Duty in respect of the following clauses—

Please fill in the details where required, in the clauses in respect of which a claim is made and cross out those clauses which do not apply—

I/We declare that—

(1) I/We hold Second-Hand Motor Vehicle Dealers Licence No._____ and am/are engaged in the business of selling motor vehicles. The vehicle will be used in the ordinary course of business for the purpose of sale or demonstration

(2) The vehicle has been aquired by—_____
(Repossession, Termination of Hiring, etc.)

(3) The vehicle described over has seating for not less than 12 adult passengers and is to be used exclusively or principally in the carriage of passengers for reward

(4) The vehicle described over will be wholly or mainly used for the transport of the applicant in consequence of the loss of the use of one/both legs. I am permanently unable to use public transport. I do not own any other vehicle on which an exemption from stamp duty has been granted. A medical certificate is produced herewith

(5) Stamp duty in respect of the vehicle described herein has been paid on another instrument which is produced herewith

(6) I am entitled to the vehicle under the terms of the will/estate of—_____
(Name of Deceased)

Date........................   F5214   *Signature of Applicant*........................

of going to your local library and asking to join. You will be given a card then and there; some of these cards can be very impressive, resembling credit cards.

"In case of accident" card: These cards often come free when you buy a wallet, or they can be purchased from most stationers. The cards are completed by the holder who writes in the name of someone he wishes notified in the event he is involved in an accident.

Club membership card: These are obtained once you join the relevant club. Note that some of these clubs run checks on applicants. Stick to "soft" clubs—shopping discount clubs, sports clubs, knitting circle clubs, etc. Unless you want to attract attention to yourself, avoid carrying cards identifying you as a member of any particular political party or firearms club.

There are hundreds of other possibilities, and most of them will end up in your pockets without much effort on your part as you gradually progress along the new identity road. In the early stages especially, hang on to all the bits of paper, cards, etc., you collect, however insignificant they might seem at the time. You never know when they might be of use.

MAILING ADDRESSES— FACT AND FICTION

Anyone who intends to apply for documents or services that may be refused—thereby generating a negative record somewhere—should use an address different from that at which he resides or works. Similarly, if you do not want a company or organization with which you are in contact to know your true whereabouts, you should use a mailing address.

You can make someone believe that you live in a wealthy part of town or that the address is that of a company or business. Many mailing-address firms offer a telephone answering service, telex facilities, and so on—all of which can be used to create the desired illusion. However, most—if not all—of these "purpose-built" companies have to advertise in order to attract business. This means that anyone can easily find out whether or not the address and number given by an individual is genuine or that of an answering service.

Some companies are, of course, more professional than others and will take steps to ensure that a caller is unable to determine whether the person to whom he is speaking is a representative of an answering service or other company. Others are less reliable and, although they may lead potential customers to believe that the service is secure, they will not risk criminal prosecution by going out of their way to mislead a caller.

To prove the above-noted point, I chose at random two advertised mailing/answering services from each of the major states or areas in the countries covered within this book and enlisted their services. The fees were very reasonable, but this might be an indication of how much reliability one can place on such services. After a reasonable time had elapsed and after I had sent a couple of letters for redirection and had some friends call the number I had been given to set the scene, I called the numbers myself and explained that I was "Inspector X" from the local police department. I told the operator at each office that we had apprehended a known criminal and that he had given this number as that of his place of work. We had reason to believe that the number was one of several used by "X Answering Services," and could they confirm this?

To no one's surprise, they *all* admitted that they were employees of an answering/mail-redirection service and that the number was indeed that of their office.

Now, any investigator worth his salt would use similar techniques—assuming there was sufficient justification. So if you *really* want to be safe, *do not* use advertised services.

In many situations, no one will bother to try to disprove the information pertaining to addresses that you supply. They will write or call, and having received a satisfactory reply will proceed with issuing your document or supplying the requested service. Give some thought as to how deeply you yourself would delve into similar information if the roles were reversed. What would it take to satisfy *you* that someone was who he claimed to be?

As a general guide, consider the following. Any legitimate business would want as many people as possible to know its phone number and address. So, if the number given as being that of an established company cannot be found in any directory or business guide, what would you conclude?

Any telephone operator who is employed in a professional capacity will give the name of the company to the caller as soon as she or he answers to call. Few, if any, will simply say, "Hello." If your call was answered in the latter fashion, what would you think?

Finally, if you called a number and asked the person who answered to identify the company you've reached and the operator seems extremely reluctant to name a company, what would you think?

All the above situations are common indications that the number is that of an answering service, or at best, a large switchboard. Incidentally, the excuse that the caller has got through to a switchboard serving several different companies is often used by answering-service employees who are trying hard not to give the game away.

Official Mail-Redirection Services

Most countries, including those covered within this book, operate a postal system which provides a redirection service for people who have recently moved from their established home address. The service is also available to persons who are staying away from home for any length of time but require the delivery of their mail as it arrives rather than waiting until their return to collect it.

Persons using the service are required to complete an application form available from the local post office. The information required varies from place to place, but an example form—which is typical of the majority used—is given below. Without exception, all official redirection services generate records of the person using the service, their old address, new permanent or temporary address, and the dates of redirection. Although this will probably be a bad thing in most circumstances, the system is a great way of generating name and address information that you *want* others to know!

Poste Restante Addresses

Upon checking with most major post offices in the countries covered here, I learned that they will all hold mail for persons whose mail is addressed in care of the post office in question without requiring that prior arrangements be made. This service, for which there is no charge, is known as *poste restante*. Providing you do not abuse this service by having scores of letters sent to the same office, there is no enforced limit on how long you may use this system. The staff at some of these offices will be more accommodating than at others, of course, so use some common sense in your frequency of use.

All offices I contacted explained that some kind of identification is required before the letter will be handed over, but the offices were not particular as to what form of identification was presented. (See the section on supportive identification.)

Safe Addresses

The preceding sections have illustrated some of the commonly used ways to divert mail in order to avoid creating accurate name/address records or to create the illusion of an established, stable background or identity. It can be seen, however, that most of these techniques rely to some extent upon the gullibility of those who process the application or submitted information, and that if these persons—credit controllers, investigators, or issuing-department representatives—bother to do their job thoroughly, the attempted deception will be discovered. However, there are ways that fictional home addresses or places of employment/businesses can be established so that they may not be disproven except in extreme circumstances.

Such techniques are simple in design but take a litle longer to set up. It may be that this extra time is the reason why many people opt for quicker, yet less secure, methods. Believe me, any extra time and effort spent in establishing a solid address will be repaid handsomely in the future.

In fact, it is not an accommodation or mailing address which provides the required degree of security, but rather a genuine address—technically at least. Quite simply, one searches the classified ads of a newpaper of a given area and selects any of the hundreds of "bed sit" or "flatlet"-type accommodations that are available. England and Australia have hundreds of thousands of these vacant properties for lease, while New Zealand has fewer. The majority of these bed-sit-type places are owned by private landlords who do not live on the premises. The tenant turnover is high, and no one but the fussiest of owners asks for references. Those that do rarely check them out.

Once you have secured an address and gone through the motions of moving in, you can apply to be placed on the electoral register, getting your name onto other files and records (detailed elsewhere).

Business addresses are just as easy to obtain.

The Post Office

P 944
(Revd 1981)

Royal Mail Redirection Service

Important notes you should read before completing this form

1 The Post Office will redirect your mail from premises which you have occupied or rented provided they were not an Hotel, Boarding House, Club, University, Lodgings or similar establishment. **Seven** days notice should be given before initial redirection is to begin, by taking or posting this form, completed, to the post office serving the district of your old address.

2 A separate fee is payable for each different surname and/or business name.

3 Additional postage may be due when letters are redirected abroad. The Post Office does not undertake to redirect abroad by air mail.

4 Parcels may be redirected to an **inland address only.** A surcharge equal to the original postage is generally payable on each parcel on delivery.

5 You may select initial periods of redirection of:

A Up to one calendar month
B Up to three calendar months
C Up to twelve calendar months.

If you later require your mail to be redirected beyond the period for which you originally paid, you must apply for an extension of the redirection period using a fresh form P944. If you do not do this, the redirection of your mail will stop. An application to extend a period of redirection should be made **before** the expiry date of the existing redirection order. The period of renewal however, **cannot commence before the period of the existing redirection has expired.**

Extension periods are available as follows:

D For a period of up to three calendar months (the period of renewal commencing **within twelve months** of the date the initial redirection order was taken out).

   (Subject to a maximum of three renewals)

E For a period of up to twelve calendar months (the period of renewal commencing **within twelve months** of the date the initial redirection order was taken out).

F For a period of up to twelve calendar months (applicable only where period of renewal commences after redirection has already been in operation for twelve months or more).

6 Payment of the fees due may be made by cheque (made payable to 'The Post Office'), by Girobank transfer for credit to the Head Postmaster's Girobank account, (please ask at the post office if you do not know the account number) or in postage stamps of the appropriate value which should be affixed in the space provided on the application form, and cancelled in ink with your signature. Information concerning the current fees for the Royal Mail Redirection Service is available at all post offices.

7 Further information you may need to know.

Mail for deceased persons, bankrupts, and people who are mentally ill will be redirected only if certain conditions are met. Details are available from your local Head Postmaster, whose address may be obtained from any post office.

The normal limit for redirecting mail from a Poste Restante address is one month.

Holders of Premium Savings Bonds should ask the post office for a change of address form P2767B and an envelope, unless they have already been issued with a Holder's Number card. These are being issued over a period of years in alphabetical order of surname.

If you do not use the Royal Mail Redirection Service, but still want details of your television licence transferred to your new address, please take your licence to any post office for amendment.

Sample of a mail-redirection service form.

The Post Office

Royal Mail Redirection Service

The Postmaster

Please redirect mail as indicated

Please read Note 2

1 Names of persons requiring redirection

Name or names (State title Mr/Mrs etc and initials)

Please use capital letters

Title	Initials	Surname	Signature

For firms, the business name should be shown followed by the signature of the Secretary or other authorised person. For households, all persons **must** give a signature.

(Warning: Criminal diversion of postal packets from an addressee is an offence under Section 56 of the PO Act 1953. The penalty is a fine not exceeding £500 or imprisonment for a term not exceeding six months or both.)

2 Address to which mail should be redirected

Please use capital letters

Old address (in full):

New address (in full):

Postcode

Postcode

Please read Note 5 for detailed explanation of options available

3 Period of redirection required

Please tick the appropriate box

applications for an initial redirection period   A   B   C

applications for extended redirection   D   E   F

Fee payable £

4 Amendment to the address on your television licence

Please complete this section in CAPITAL LETTERS if your change of address is permanent and you want details of your television licence transferred to your new address.

Name shown on licence:

Old address shown on licence:

New address:

Postcode

Postcode

Television licences are not transferable from one person to another, but if you are changing your name on marriage please enter your new name here.

Change of name:

P944 (Revd 1981)

please turn over

5 Starting date

Redirection is to start from						19

If the change of address is temporary,
please also give the finishing date					19

6 Parcels

See Note 4

Please tick this box if you require parcels to be redirected. If this box is left blank parcels will be treated as undeliverable and returned to sender(s)

7 Fees

See Note 6

I wish to pay the fee due by (please delete as appropriate):

a Cheque made payable to 'The Post Office'.
b Girobank transfer to the Head Postmaster's Girobank account.
c Postage stamps which are affixed in the space below and cancelled with my signature.

8 I note that The Post Office reserves the right to refuse to redirect mail and/or to discontinue this redirection order at any time.

Signature								19

For official use only

Office date stamp

For completion at the delivery office serving old address

1 Request recorded on P553B	2 Acknowledgement letter sent	3 Sent to Postcode Duty	4 (if applicable) Recorded in Accounts Branch for payment to Subpostmaster
Initials	Initials	Initials	Initials
Date	Date	Date	Date

Retention period: 1 year after expiry date

Do not detach

For attention at Delivery Office serving old address

Send complete form to Postcode Duty.

For attention at Postcode Duty

Check Postcode details, detach this section and forward it to
National TV Licence Records Office, BRISTOL BS98 1TL.

For attention at NTVLRO

Transfer licence details from old to new address and change name if necessary.

There are plenty of office spaces to rent on a short-term basis (even monthly) in the majority of Commonwealth countries. Large companies will often sublet some of their office space in order to recoup some of the rent and rates they themselves are paying. Therefore, it is possible to secure a prestigious address for a minimal outlay. Many such sublets offer telephone and telex services as well as typing and copying facilities. However, in *this* instance, they are genuine! The telephone operator will really be working for you, not an answering service.

With access to genuine private and business addresses so easy to obtain—and relatively inexpensively—I cannot for the life of me understand why people bother to use false addresses. After all, basing a new identity on fake information is just looking for trouble.

Even if your requirements are short-term, it is still safer to obtain a genuine address and use it until it has served its purpose. You may have to pay a month's rent for just one week's use, but the extra cost is, in my opinion, worth it. It is a simple matter to have a friend answer incoming calls and give the information you tell him to give out, or to use a call diverter to reroute the calls.

In fact, the only time I would recommend using a mailing address proper is when it is impossible for you to get to the area in question to spend some time setting things up.

PHONE-CALL DIVERTERS

Use of phone-call diverters, also known as line switchers, is prohibited by many telephone authorities unless the user can prove the need for such a system (as in a business situation, for example, where the diverter can be used to switch an incoming call to a phone in a different office or section of the factory if the original number called is not answered within a given period of time). In England, these diverters are illegal.

The operation is completely automatic, and these devices should not be confused with personnel-controlled switchboard systems.

The beauty of these diverters is that they can be programmed to switch the incoming call to any other number without the caller's knowledge. For example, you may have applied for a credit card and on the application form given the number of your employer as 321-1235. This is a downtown number and corresponds to your employer's address. Both the name and address of the employer are fictitious. The number is in actuality that of a downtown basement apartment you have rented solely for the purpose of obtaining the credit card. The call diverter could be programmed to switch the incoming call to, say, 765-5888, the number of the real apartment in which you are staying. This apartment might be in a different part of the city, different town, or even a completely different part of the world!

If the credit company were to call, the first check the credit checker would make would be to ensure the number and supposed location of the company you claimed to work for matched correctly. Many amateur fraud artists make the stupid mistake of giving a telephone number that *does not* match the supposed location of their work place.

When the 321-1235 number is dialed, the call diverter will automatically redial the 765-5888 number. You might arrange to have this call answered by a friend, who acts the part of the company telephone operator who can call you to the phone or confirm that you work there if so required. You may prefer to prerecord a message for the answering machine: something to the effect that the company is closed for lunch, requesting the caller phone back in thirty minutes.

BANK ACCOUNTS

A current, regular checking account can be easily opened at most banks upon production of some basic identification. If you have a driver's license, so much the better; if you don't, a letter, service bill, club membership card, or rent-book will usually suffice. The type of I.D. accepted depends on the exclusivity of the bank and the attitude of the staff person with whom you are dealing. Many banks in England, Australia, and New Zealand require potential customers to furnish two references. Some banks insist that these referees have accounts of their own at the same bank, but the majority of banks seem prepared to accept references from anyone who will sign a declaration to the effect that they have known the applicant for a certain amount of years and believe him to be capable of maintaining a bank account. Although there is often no minimum limit on the time that referees must have known the applicant, it is obvious that the greater the length of time that can be claimed, the better.

In practice, it will be found that many banks waive the referee requirement, and it is possible to enter a bank, explain your situation, and open an account then and there with a few pounds. The checkbook will usually be sent to you later through the mail. It is best to choose a busy day on which to open your account if you are trying to do so without references at a bank that usually requires them; aim for the youngest, most inexperienced-looking clerk. If you are a male, go to a female clerk, and vice versa. I once opened an account at a high-street bank in London, using the clerk and her sister as referees! I did not know them when I entered the bank—but we soon made friends!

When you give the names of your referees, if so required, the bank will frequently send out statement forms to them immediately. These forms are standard and simple, and the bank makes no further contact with the referees unless you vanish one day leaving a massive overdraft. Once the referees return the forms, your checkbook will be issued.

Do not worry if you can't find anyone to act as a referee for you. You can rent a couple of cheap apartments before approaching the bank, giving the addresses of the apartments as those of your "referees." As far as I can establish, no other checks are made by the bank to determine whether the people and addresses you give are genuine. All banks will require you to give a specimen signature. If you are not used to your new identification, practice a signature until it becomes second nature, and then stick with it.

If you cannot afford to rent a couple of addresses, you can select them from the local area and give a fictitious name with each to serve as your referees. Assume the statement form will be sent by the bank the same day you apply for an account or the day after at the latest. Be in a position to intercept the mailman as he delivers the letters to those addresses. Obviously you will need to enlist the services of a friend for this one, unless you can run *really* fast!

When the mailman makes his delivery, knock on the door of the residence and explain, apologetically, that you think you have given the wrong house number to (whoever you like) and inquire as to whether any mail has arrived there for you. I put this technique to the test a few months back and it worked really well. It does have its drawbacks, of course, but if you choose the address carefully—and as an extra security measure, cross-reference it in a local directory to make sure the occupant isn't the bank manager—you will have no trouble. To be even safer, choose an address from which the occupants are about to move (watch for the "For Sale/Sold" signs). Yet another technique is to give the address of an *empty* house that is for sale, and get the keys from the real estate agent on the day of the mail delivery in order to rescue your letters. This method is used quite a lot in Australia, I hear. Apparently, certain people secure an address in such a manner and then have hire-purchase goods delivered there. They make sure they are around to meet the delivery man and sign for the goods, and then they disappear. What will they think of next?

Many of the major banks are adopting computerized withdrawal and deposit systems. This means that one can put money in or take it out of an account at any hour of the day or night, without having to actually enter the bank and speak with any of the employees. It is all done via those hole-in-the-wall machines or electronic tellers. Such systems are ideal for the individual who prefers a degree of anonymity. Once you have opened your account, the bank will automatically send you details of such systems.

Taxation

The income-tax system in the Commonwealth is quite different from that in the United States, but suffice it to say here that in the United States, it is *far* harder to "lose" money or to avoid having one's banking details checked and referenced. Having said that, it is very possible that countries not already doing so will follow England in its change of attitude toward income earned from bank accounts. At the time of writing, a change was being introduced into the tax-collection system which requires that the tax on interest from bank accounts be paid *directly* to the government by the bank (as opposed to having the individual declare such income on his tax-return form). How this affects individuals will vary according to the amount of tax they already pay. Financial implications aside, it shows that the trend is toward wider dissemination of personal information, or, at the least, removal of the "individual factor." As previously mentioned, I think this trend is a good thing, making for easier exploitation of the system by individuals who know how to play the game!

I contacted several banks in all of the countries covered herein, and the bottom line is that you

GENERAL TECHNIQUES AND INFORMATION

have a chat with a bank manager. He *will* be pleased to help (assuming you have something he wants—money) and *is* familiar with the "legal" ways of maintaining anonymity and avoiding tax hassles. I also found several managers who said they were prepared to open accounts for individuals "with the necessary requirements" without the need for any of the usual "formalities!" I dare not include the names and addresses of the banks here, but it serves to illustrate that if you ask, you might be pleasantly surprised. If you do not ask, you will never know.

Building Society Accounts

The sample application form below shows how easy it is to open a building society account in England. Name, address, and specimen signature are all that are required—plus a little hard cash, of course—and away you go. *No* checking or cross-referencing; *no* referees or guarantors. The tax is deducted at the source. Most building societies will also provide a checkbook in order that a third party may be paid by the account holder without the need for cash to change hands. Also, as can be seen in the example below, interest can be transferred by the society to a bank account or sent to an address nominated by the holder. Limitations on the total amount which may be kept in one account do exist. (In the example below, the limit is £30,000.) The amount which can be withdrawn without notice is restricted. Even so, as a way of storing funds which earn higher than normal interest and ensuring that you have some very solid identification, building societies rate highly.

If you opt for such an account, I suggest you open several different accounts and keep the total funds in each one well below the maximum limit. By doing so, you will not attract unwanted interest from the Inland Revenue; if anything untoward should happen, you will always have other funds to fall back on. *No evidential identification is required when opening such accounts.*

OBTAINING CREDIT CARDS AND ESTABLISHING A GOOD CREDIT RECORD

Obtaining a credit card or credit facilities is not in itself sufficient to generate a good credit record. Many people obtain credit and then fall behind with their payments. The close links which exist

---

CHELTENHAM GOLD ACCOUNT

Your savings will start earning interest the day we receive this application, so please complete it using block letters and send it with your initial investment to C & G at the address overleaf.

SURNAME (Mr. Mrs. or Miss) FIRST NAMES

ADDRESS

POSTCODE

(\ appropriate boxes)
I am ☐ am not ☐ an existing C & G investor

Please invest £ _____ in a CHELTENHAM GOLD ACCOUNT. I/We would like the interest added to the account to earn even more interest.

I/We hereby agree to be bound by the Society's Rules.
I/We make the declaration specified overleaf.

For accounts in joint names (excluding Trust Accounts) the Society is authorised to accept
☐ ANY ONE }
☐ ALL   } of our signatures as a discharge for withdrawals.

(Where applicable) I/We invest as Trustees/Administrators/Executors of

Signed

Dated

Only complete this section if you do not wish your interest to be added to your account.
I/We would like the interest
☐ paid to

☐ paid into Bank Account No.
with _____ Bank
at
Sort code

Sample application form for opening a building society account.

---

between credit agencies ensure that most, if not all, credit companies operating in the area get to know about the "bad debtor" in a very short time. Eventually other companies may be so notified. This means that a hundred doors can be slammed in your face even before you get the chance to knock on them. Similarly, having a credit card which you never use can also generate a negative record.

Some thought should be given as to what types

of credit services you join, and I recommend that you start small.

Mail-order Companies

Mail-order catalogs, popular in all the countries covered by this book, illustrate a wide range of goods, all of which can be purchased with "interest-free credit." (The prices of these goods are in actuality inflated to take into account this lack of computed interest.)

All catalog companies send out invitations to people whose names they get either from the electoral register or from companies who specialize in selling such names and addresses. Also, I know for a fact that one major English company sends catalog invitations to people whose names appear in the telephone directory. Such letters usually include the words, "or occupier," in addition to the addressee's name, just in case he or she has moved or their information is incorrect. Once you have been a resident at an address for a few months, and especially if you register to vote or have a telephone installed, you can guarantee that a catalog invitation will arrive in the mail before too long.

The beauty of these catalogs is that the information you need to supply in order to be accepted as an agent is minimal. (The catalog system operates by allowing the person who has applied for the catalog, the agent, to buy goods themselves or sell to others on a commission basis.) Very often, all you will be asked is your name, address, occupation, and age. *No* checks are made in England as far as I can determine, and the checks are very basic in Australia and New Zealand.

Such companies can afford to be lax in checking applicants, since their profits and insurance more than compensate for any rip-offs, and the value of goods ordered by a new applicant is restricted to a reasonable amount until the applicant has proven to be trustworthy. I have seen catalogs issued to countless "unreal" persons over the years, confirming the fact that the majority of such companies do not bother to check the information supplied on the application form *except* perhaps to confirm that the applicant is a registered voter.

Voter Registration—General Information

Getting your name on electoral registers is easy. If you are in the country long enough and use a regular address, an application will likely fall through your mailbox. If not, applications can be obtained by writing to the applicable department, the address of which will be found in any directory.

Since checking the electoral register is one method by which credit companies and other organizations confirm an individual's identity claim, voter registration should be considered of prime importance by the clean-slater. It is in fact an offense in many countries—punishable by a fine or worse—to not register and/or vote. In such areas, *not* being on the register would arouse some suspicion, and the attendant interest generated would do little to help any would-be fresh start.

English Electoral Registration

The English Electoral Register is a computerized system, notorious for "creating" nonexistent people. No cross-referencing exists, and it is common for two voting cards to be sent to the same address (one showing the registered person as, for example, Mr. T. Hooper, and the other as Mr. T. Hoopor). Computer hiccups, or clerk typos, are responsible for such errors, and I suspect that the same thing happens in many other countries where the system relies on technology to collate, file, and issue similar documents with no manual check being made. Of course, a large work volume means that manual checks are not possible; as the use of such technology grows, so will the incidence of error and the ease of abuse.

As we are discussing credit and money in general here, it is worth noting that a certain finance/loan company operating in England at this time will grant a loan of several hundred pounds over the counter, so to speak, to applicants who can supply proof of earnings (a couple of pay slips), proof of identity (a license or birth certificate), and proof of address (inclusion on the electoral register). That's all—no checks, no cross-referencing. You can walk in, show the required identification, and walk out ten minutes later with the cash. Doing so will kill two birds with one stone: you thereby raise some capital and create a positive credit record, assuming you repay the loan as required. The company is well known and advertises regularly on television. I dare not give the company's name herein in the context of new identification, but stroll casually down any high

GENERAL TECHNIQUES AND INFORMATION

street in any major city, and you will find the name yourself.

Come to think of it, you can kill *three* birds with one stone by utilizing such simple loan facilities, acquiring the money, credit record, *and* the loan repayment book, which in itself is great identification.

The English Electoral Register application (shown herein) and accompanying instructions/requirements are available in English only. For your interest, the Electoral Rights information pamphlet supplied by the Australian government gives details in English, Italian, Greek, Vietnamese, Serbian, Turkish, Spanish, Arabic, Croatian, Chinese, and Polish!

Credit Card Application

The conditions you will have to meet before

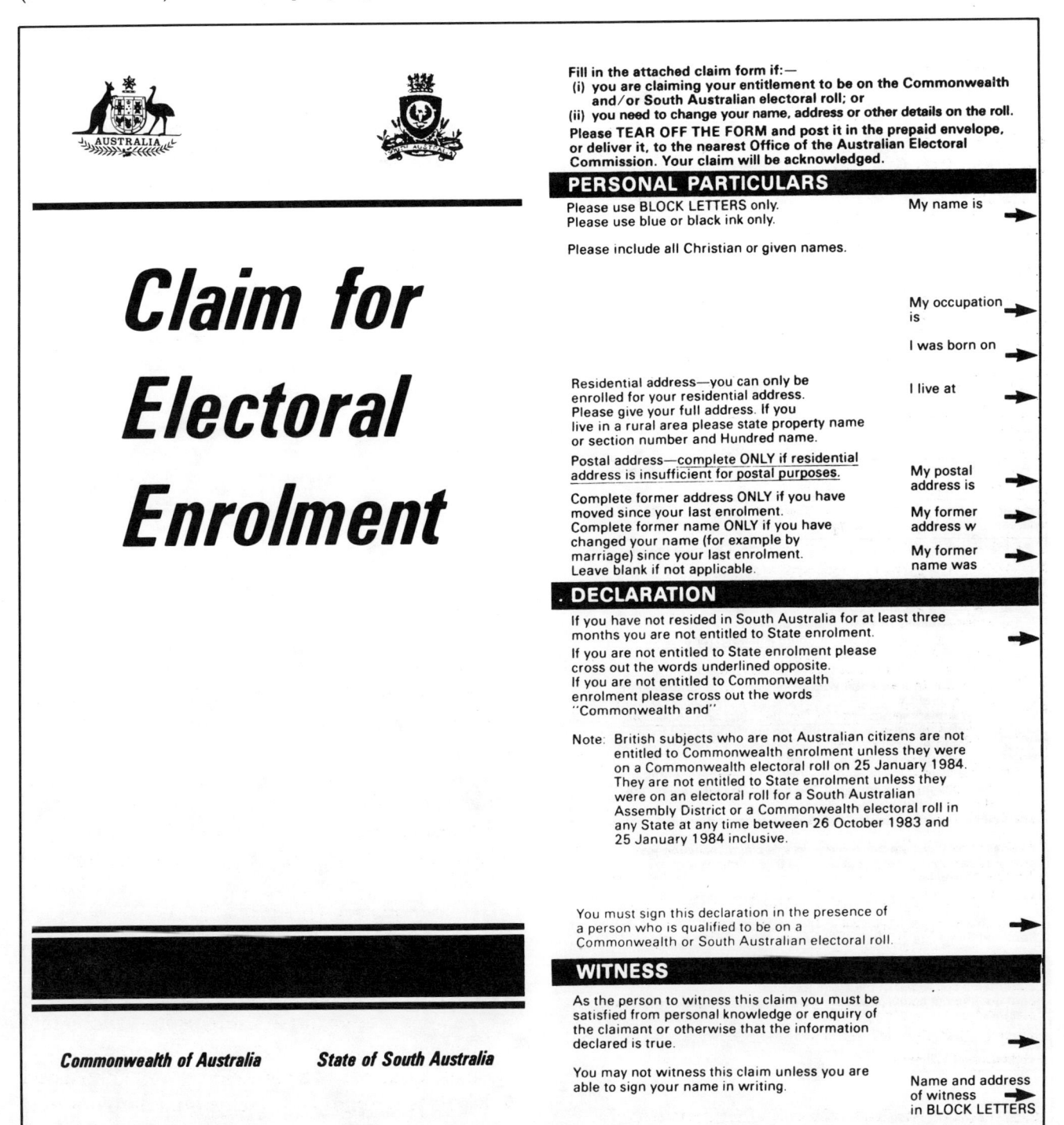

Claim for Electoral Enrolment

Commonwealth of Australia   State of South Australia

Fill in the attached claim form if:—
(i) you are claiming your entitlement to be on the Commonwealth and/or South Australian electoral roll; or
(ii) you need to change your name, address or other details on the roll.
Please TEAR OFF THE FORM and post it in the prepaid envelope, or deliver it, to the nearest Office of the Australian Electoral Commission. Your claim will be acknowledged.

PERSONAL PARTICULARS

Please use BLOCK LETTERS only.
Please use blue or black ink only.

Please include all Christian or given names.

My name is →

My occupation is →

I was born on →

Residential address—you can only be enrolled for your residential address. Please give your full address. If you live in a rural area please state property name or section number and Hundred name.

I live at →

Postal address—complete ONLY if residential address is insufficient for postal purposes.

My postal address is →

Complete former address ONLY if you have moved since your last enrolment.
Complete former name ONLY if you have changed your name (for example by marriage) since your last enrolment.
Leave blank if not applicable.

My former address w →

My former name was →

DECLARATION

If you have not resided in South Australia for at least three months you are not entitled to State enrolment.

If you are not entitled to State enrolment please cross out the words underlined opposite.
If you are not entitled to Commonwealth enrolment please cross out the words "Commonwealth and"

Note: British subjects who are not Australian citizens are not entitled to Commonwealth enrolment unless they were on a Commonwealth electoral roll on 25 January 1984. They are not entitled to State enrolment unless they were on an electoral roll for a South Australian Assembly District or a Commonwealth electoral roll in any State at any time between 26 October 1983 and 25 January 1984 inclusive.

You must sign this declaration in the presence of a person who is qualified to be on a Commonwealth or South Australian electoral roll.

WITNESS

As the person to witness this claim you must be satisfied from personal knowledge or enquiry of the claimant or otherwise that the information declared is true.

You may not witness this claim unless you are able to sign your name in writing.

Name and address of witness → in BLOCK LETTERS

South Australian Electoral Roll Application

being issued a credit card vary from country to country and depend, in part, on how many people hold the cards already and the card's exclusivity. (An Amex card is harder to get, for example, than an Access, or Visa card.)

Access cards are very easy to obtain, providing you give the right information on the application form. Once again, the "right" information will vary, but close examination of the application form will show you just what you should write in. For example, if the application asks you to state the number of years you have lived at your current address and then asks for your previous address *if* the first answer was less than three years, you will always put that you have been at your current address for (at least) three years.

Other important factors to consider are as follows:

Batch No.	SD Code	I.N.		Official Use Date Rec'd

Commonwealth of Australia   State of South Australia

Surname				
All Christian or given names				
Occupation		and I am (tick one)	Male	Female
day month year / /	in	Town	Country	
Flat/House number		Street/Road		
Suburb/Town/Locality			Postcode	
Postal address			Postcode	
Former address	No.	Street	Suburb/Town	State/Territory
Former surname (if applicable)		Former Christian or given names		

I am entitled to enrolment as a Commonwealth <u>and State of South Australia</u> elector because
  (a) I have attained 18 years of age; and
  (b) <u>I have lived continuously in South Australia for at least 3 months</u>; and
  (c) I am an Australian citizen (OR a British subject who:
    (i) on 25 January 1984 was enrolled on a Commonwealth electoral roll; <u>and/or</u>,
    (ii) at sometime between 26 October 1983 and 25 January 1984 inclusive was enrolled on an electoral roll for a South Australian Assembly District or a Commonwealth electoral roll in any State); and
  (d) I have lived at my present address (or elsewhere within the Subdivision) for a period of one month immediately before the date of this claim,
and I claim enrolment for the Subdivision where I now live.

I declare that the statements made in this claim, including my personal particulars set out above, are true to the best of my knowledge and belief.

.... / /
Personal Signature or Mark of Claimant   Date

I saw this claim signed by the claimant and am satisfied that the statements contained in the claim are true.
I am qualified to be enrolled on a Commonwealth or South Australian electoral roll.

....
Signature of Witness
Name
Address

NOTE
Special Commonwealth enrolment can be obtained by:—
- persons who are 17 years of age and who would like provisional enrolment before they turn 18;
- persons going overseas for an extended period; and
- persons with no permanent place of living in Australia.

Special Commonwealth provisions can apply to persons who, because of a severe physical handicap, are unable to sign a claim for electoral enrolment.

You will find information about these provisions in the Australian Electoral Commission pamphlets, or you should contact any Office of the Australian Electoral Commission for further information.

C. J. THOMPSON, Commonwealth Government Printer

BIRMINGHAM

THE OCCUPIER

If undelivered return to:
Electoral Registration Officer,
102 New Street, Birmingham B2 4HJ

POSTAGE PAID BIRMINGHAM SERIAL No. 31

Register of Electors 1984

Representation of the People Acts

Register of Electors 1984

FORM A

Representation of the People Acts

Register in force for twelve months from 16th February 1984

Qualifying date 10th October 1983

No one may vote at elections to Parliament, local councils or the European Assembly unless his/her name appears in a register of electors. A new register is produced each year and **the law requires the householder to supply the information necessary to ensure that all eligible persons are included.**

The information required is shown on the form overleaf. Please complete, sign and return it as quickly as possible. **Do not wait until 10th October.**

You should complete the form even if you intend to move house after 10th October 1983.

If no one in the household is eligible to be included in the register, please write 'NONE' and return the form.

REMEMBER Only those in a Register of Electors are entitled to vote

HMSO 56-3543

2

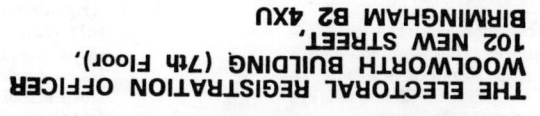

BUSINESS REPLY SERVICE
Licence No. BM 3167

THE ELECTORAL REGISTRATION OFFICER
WOOLWORTH BUILDING (7th Floor),
102 NEW STREET,
BIRMINGHAM B2 4XU

Do not affix Postage Stamp if posted in Gt. Britain, Channel Islands, N. Ireland or the Isle of Man

Postage will be paid by licensee

1984 Electoral Register application.

REGISTER OF ELECTORS 1984

Address

No. of flat, room or floor (where applicable)	No. of house (or name if not numbered)	Name of street or road	Remainder of address including post code

Names
Enter below all British citizens, other Commonwealth citizens and citizens of the Irish Republic eligible to vote, who are or will be 18 or over before 16th February 1985. (See instruction below)

Surname and title (Mr, Mrs, Miss etc.) (BLOCK LETTERS)	Full Christian names or forenames (BLOCK LETTERS)	16/17 YEAR OLDS Give date of birth of those born between 17th February 1966 and 15th February 1967 inclusive. (See the instructions below)	If merchant seaman enter a ✓	JURY SERVICE (see note 2) If over 65 by 16th February 1984 enter a ✓

Other Residents
Is any part of your house or flat *separately* occupied by persons not entered above?   *Please answer Yes or No.*

Declaration
I declare that to the best of my knowledge and belief the particulars given above are true and accurate, and that all those whose names are entered above are *British citizens, other Commonwealth citizens or citizens of the Irish Republic,* will be 18 or over by 15th February, 1985, and are eligible to be included in the register of electors.

Sign here: .... Date..

Instructions

1 You are required to enter the names of all those eligible to vote. These are British citizens, other Commonwealth citizens and citizens of the Irish Republic who will be resident at your address on 10th October 1983 and who are 18 or will become 18 while the register is in use.

Remember to include —
(a) those who are only 16 or 17 now but who will become 18 before 16th February 1985.
They will be eligible to vote as soon as they are 18;
(b) all British citizens, British Dependent Territories citizens, British Overseas citizens and citizens of other Commonwealth countries;
(c) those who normally live at your address but are temporarily away, for example on holiday; as students; in hospital (including voluntary patients in psychiatric hospitals); or as reservists called up for service or training;
(d) any residents, except short stay guests, at your address (which may be, for example a hostel or club), including merchant seamen who live there when not at sea;
(e) anyone who is away working, unless his/her absence will be for more than six months.

2 Do not include the following, for whom special arrangements are made—
(a) members of HM Forces:
(b) wives or husbands of members of HM Forces **who have made a service declaration which they have not cancelled;**
(c) Crown servants employed outside the United Kingdom;
(d) British Council staff employed outside the United Kingdom;
(e) wives or husbands of Crown servants or British Council staff employed outside the United Kingdom **if living abroad** to be with their husbands or wives.

notes
POSTAL VOTING
1 *Postal votes are available for certain persons who may have difficulty in voting in person. These include the blind, the disabled, those leaving the area, and those whose work regularly takes them away from home.*
Contact the local council for more information.
JURY SERVICE
2 *Electors who are over 65 are ineligible on age grounds for jury service. Those who are ineligible on other grounds will be able to say so if they receive a jury summons.*

MOISTEN THIS STRIP AND REFOLD FORM WHERE INDICATED SO THAT RETURN ADDRESS IS TO VIEW

- *Age*
  Twenty-two to fifty-five years of age seems to be the age range most of the companies I contacted prefer.
- *Marital status*
  Being married indicates more stability than being single.
- *Employment status*
  A professional is considered a better risk than a manual worker. However, your income will override this consideration in most cases.
- *Other financial commitments*
  The more of your income that is left over after you pay out other commitments, the better. (After all, the company does not want you to stop paying *it* in order to pay your other debts!)
- *Bank account*
  A person *without* a bank account is considered a poor risk by almost all credit companies. There are exceptions, however.
- *Home telephone*
  Having a telephone indicates to the company that you can be contacted quickly should the need arise. It also enables the company to place a check call to immediately determine whether you really do live where you claim!
- *Income*
  In today's financial climate, especially in England and other Commonwealth countries, an individual's net income is usually the prime factor in encouraging a credit company to grant credit. In England, for example, it is quite common for a dustman (sanitation worker) to earn twice the wage of a white-collar worker. Therefore, a driver/laborer with an income of £300 per week is more likely to be granted credit than an assistant manager in an insurance office who only earns £150 per week in hard cash. A manual worker who is employed by a local council or a company with powerful union connections is considered a better risk than someone who, although they may hold a more "upmarket" job, has a higher risk of being laid off.

There are very few credit companies in England, Australia, and New Zealand which ask for information as personal as that required by American organizations. I have seen credit-application forms from the United States that require the applicant to give his height, weight—even eye color. This sort of thing would never be tolerated in England,

Companies advertising loans such as this typical "no-contact" loan are usually true to their word and will not contact the applicant's employers.

and the average Australian's comments regarding such questions in that context are unprintable!

I must emphasize again the need to *use* the card once you get it. Just having the card will not produce enough positive evidence of your ability to pay regularly. Once you have one card, you will probably find that other companies (who have bought your personal details from the original company) will write to you and offer you *their* credit card without any fuss. Sometimes they will even offer you a preapproved credit limit—based on information you gave to the other company! The application you receive in this case will be treated as a formality, and checks will only be made to see whether you are on the electoral register. It is very rare for any of the major credit companies to actually contact your employer, although they *might* check to see if the business is in the phone book.

Loans and Hire Purchase

Perhaps it is a sign of the times, but a great many companies are now offering loans or hire-purchase facilities, guaranteeing that they will not contact the individual's employer (a sample application is shown below). From personal experience, I can say that they check to see if the company you claim to work for is listed in the phone book or trade directory, but they *will not* make contact. I recently had a credit controller from a company I had contacted for a credit-purchase phone me at home. Try as I might, I could not think of a way to avoid speaking with him and still get the credit, but I took a deep breath and returned his call. It turned out that he wanted me to explain why the employer I listed on the application form was not listed in the phone book. I told him that he had not looked in the book properly; when I described exactly where in the directory the name and address could be found, he was satisfied. It occurred to me sometime later that he must have been able to find the name but that he wanted to reassure himself I really lived where I said I did. The phone call settled the matter. If the same thing happens to you, don't panic and don't assume the worst if you are asked for more details by phone or letter.

The fact that many companies are trying to generate new customers by guaranteeing not to contact their employers means, of course, that one can easily claim to work for any company, the name of which has been pulled from a directory. The obvious mistakes to avoid include using a company that is located in the same area as the loan company, and giving your (imaginary) position within the company as that of a senior staff member. Such information can be checked easily by referring to company records, so be sure to *always* indicate a low-key occupation. Large factories or other plants employing hundreds of people are your best bets, and small firms which are likely to employ only a few people should be avoided.

Remember Your "New" Name

A common error committed by clean-slaters and other persons using newly adopted identification is that they forget what information they have given to the various companies, agencies, departments, etc. This confusion can cause obvious problems, but problems can be easily avoided if you spend a little time to keep a note of what you say to whom. It is of little use to obtain credit, buy something, and pay off the debt over the following year, thereby establishing a good credit record, if you can't remember what information you put on the original application form when you next want a loan. This happens a *lot!*

In this connection, I always recall the time when I had opened a bank account under a different name in order that I might "lose" a percentage of my income. The money I had earned had been paid into the account by my employer, and the account number had been forwarded to my home address. When the time came for me to make a withdrawal, I wandered down to the bank and filled in a withdrawal slip for the required amount, and the clerk went off to key the information into her computer. It was a lovely, sunny day, and I was looking forward to having a bit of extra cash. Suddenly, I realized everyone in the bank was looking at me, and I felt my face turn a deep shade of pink.

"Mr. Smith?" the teller called. (I have changed the names to protect the innocent.) "Yes, er, no, er," I stumbled. It turns out that I had signed the withdrawal slip in my real name instead of that in which the account had been opened!

"Are you sure your account is here, Mr. Smith?" the clerk asked. Believe me, the looks I was getting from other customers just cannot be described! I could see the shadowy figure of the bank manager stirring in the distance.

To cut a long story short, I burbled on about how I had been working nights for the last week, had no sleep, and was very tired. Apologetically, I explained that I had just bought a car from a guy named Smith, and had his name on my mind when I filled in the withdrawal slip, having just completed the ownership details for the car. They bought the story, and I filled in another slip. They seemed a bit wary, but there was not a lot they could do. Fortunately, I had supportive identification for the fake name with me, and being able to produce such I.D. probably helped smooth things out.

The incident showed me two things: firstly, it is important to prepare properly for such occasions, especially if you are under pressure or not feeling your best. Secondly, it proved that you can get away with anything if you think quickly and do not panic.

Book or Magazine Offers

Another surefire way of getting your new name on the majority of credit or general-information computers cheaply and simply is to reply to one of the many offers you get in the mail to buy a series of books or magazines over a twelve-month period. The first book is sent to you free, you examine it for ten days or so, and if you want to keep it and continue with the scheme, you send off the money. The other books will be sent to you at regular intervals, and you are usually given a week or so to pay for them. Free gifts are frequently offered which are yours to keep even if you do not want the books. A prepaid return envelope is included with the original mailing, so the whole thing is made very easy (and therefore tempting) for you. The only hassle I have found with such projects is actually fitting one's name and address into the little spaces the computer allocates for that purpose. Once you subscribe to such a scheme, you will suddenly find your name and address appearing on a variety of other offers. A great way of getting "your" name known!

RECIPROCAL AGREEMENTS

Reciprocal agreements covering a wide variety of trade, travel, and employment situations exist between England, Australia, New Zealand, and Canada.

Such agreements enable holders of passports and other I.D. documents issued in one member country to travel to and from another, spending time "abroad" with minimal restriction. Emmigration/immigration formalities are simplified, and state benefits earned in one country can often be transferred to, and redeemed in, another. Bilateral agreements also exist between certain Commonwealth countries and other, non-Commonwealth countries, an example of which are the agreements existing between Canada and the United States. Agreements such as these mean that valid identification obtained in any of the relevant countries (EEC, Commonwealth, etc.) is *extremely* valuable and useful.

So that you may best determine the areas of operation most suited to your requirements, the following notes show some of the practical aspects of this reciprocity.

English I.D.

Driver's license. The English driver's license is valid in France, Germany, Holland, and other EEC member states, and an English license can be exchanged for a license issued by these nations. The precise conditions that must be met by an applicant who wishes to exchange a license for one issued by one of these countries vary. However, in the majority of cases, claiming residence for extended periods will suffice. The English license is also valid in the United States.

State benefits (retirement, widows, etc.) earned in England can be redeemed in any of the EEC countries, as well as in Australia and New Zealand.

Passports issued to U.K. nationals are accepted by all countries except during such times as certain governments are refusing entry to British subjects. Fortunately, this happens infrequently. The U.K. visitors passport *is not* accepted by Australia or New Zealand, but it *is* accepted by the Canadian authorities providing that it is valid for at least one month *after* the last day of the visit.

As of January 1983, U.K. passports have borne the following statement (where applicable): "Holder has the right of abode in the United Kingdom." This statement secures for the holder the right to take up employment or start his own business in any EEC member-state, except Greece.

Medical card and number. Treatment under the National Health Service is available in England only. However, the EEC social security regulations entitle visitors from England to receive immediate medical treatment in any other EEC country (West Germany, France, Belgium, Denmark, Gibraltar, Holland, Italy, Luxembourg and the Irish Republic) on the same terms as privately insured citizens of that country. Obviously, it is important that one does not give the impression, in such circumstances, that the purpose of the visit was simply to obtain free medical treatment! To ensure that free or heavily subsidized medical treatment is made available to persons holding a U.K. passport, the traveler should obtain Form E11 from an English Social Security office before commencing the journey.

New Zealand Passport

The New Zealand passport is accepted by all countries. A valid passport is required to enter New Zealand, except by nationals of Australia and the Commonwealth countries who have permission to reside indefinitely in Australia and New Zealand. New Zealand citizens *do not* require a passport in order to enter Australia.

Canada/United States

Customs procedures for U.S. citizens or residents at the U.S./Canadian border crossings are extremely relaxed. It is possible to pass from one country to another upon production of some very basic identification. A driver's license, birth certificate, Social Security card, and alien green card are all acceptable.

KEEPING THE PAST AT BAY

Once you have made a fresh start and a clean break from your past, it is imperative your past be kept at bay. *Kept* being the operative word as you will have to work at staying one step ahead of those who might have reason to try to track you down. You may think that there is no one who is interested enough to want to find you, but can you be sure? Of course, if you have left debts behind or considerable ill will, you can practically guarantee that someone will try and find you. What about that long-lost friend who, upon returning to your hometown learns of your disappearance and, albeit with the best intentions, sets about trying to find you? And what about your abandoned wife's live-in-lover who might decide that the alimony a court would demand you pay could keep him in the luxury to which he could easily become accustomed? Enough said I think.

The single, most important factor in ensuring your continued freedom is *not to tell anyone* the game you intend to play. Make your plans alone, and, when you go—go! Do not leave a forwarding address with people you *think* you can trust. I have plenty of friends, some very close—but I trust *none* of them. Unless you want to fail, you must adopt this same attitude. One of Freud's theories was that all criminals deliberately, but subconsciously, leave clues; in the more obvious "cries for help," people leave plenty of clues. The most common clue offered by persons who have adopted a new identity is their reticence to change their name *completely*. Experience shows that the vast majority of such people will adopt a new surname, but retain their given Christian name, or they will keep the initial letters of their real name. Armed with such information, an investigator can check records to determine which individuals have moved into a certain area who have the same Christian name or initials as those of the person he is seeking. If you consciously avoid this error, you will have already bought yourself a useful amount of extra breathing space.

Distance

The greater the distance you can put between your old self and the new, the better. Do however, avoid—at all costs—moving to an area in which friends or relatives reside. Even if you do not make contact with them, an investigator would soon discover the link and initiate inquiries in that area. Also avoid areas that are known to be your favorites, such as places you regularly visited on vacation or during business trips.

Employment

If, like most of us, you are unfortunate enough to have to work for a living, aim for a job in the new area that is as different as possible from that which you are known to have had back home. Your pride might be an obstacle here, but if you really want to avoid detection, especially in the early stages of your new life, swallow hard and keep a low profile. This advice is of particular importance to persons who normally hold down a specialist job or provide a service on a self-employed basis.

Pastimes

Harmless enough you may think, but pastimes have been the downfall of many! Making a break with the past can, and does, clean the slate of accumulated debts, wrong-choice partners, and a multitude of other negative factors. However, along with the bad *must* go some of the good, and hobbies or pastimes should be considered on top of the list. Awhile ago, I was approached by a local shopkeeper who had been ripped off to the tune of £1500 by some guy who had passed a bad check to pay for an amateur radio rig and some ancillary equipment. The shopkeeper knew my background and felt that I might be able to help him out. Although the loss was substantial to a small business, it was not enough to justify his employing the services of a professional skiptracer. However, I agreed to help—for a small commission if successful—and set about visiting the local second-hand shops, where the majority of ripped-off goods can be found.

I spent some time looking around such shops, without any luck, so I decided to call on a friend of mine who is a licensed amateur radio operator and tell him about the shopkeeper's situation.

Having assured me that he would keep an ear to the ground for news of anyone selling radio equipment a little *too* cheaply, he set about showing me his impressive radio equipment. We were in the middle of scanning a local calling frequency, when the rig locked on to a "C.Q." call (some guy asking for a radio check). My friend answered his call, gave him a signal report, and started chatting. Surprise, surprise, this guy had just bought some new equipment and was in the process of testing it.

A few quick calls, a bit of dial twiddling, and my friend had the approximate location of our new boy to within a mile or so.

The guy seemed surprised when we knocked on his door, and positively shocked when I identified the equipment he was using as that which had been "stolen" from the shop. We never called the police about the rip-off—and the guy never called the police about the damage his face sustained. A fair deal, we thought.

This condensed story serves to illustrate the dangers of being too cocky. Had the guy simply sold the equipment or hidden it for a few months before using it, chances are that he would never have been found out. The same principle regarding cockiness applies to those of you who want to start your life over or adopt a new identity on a temporary basis.

Vehicles

Selling your '67 Mustang (or whatever vehicle you own) is a must unless you want to be found in extremely short order. Changing the ownership details is not enough, nor is reregistering the vehicle. All changes or alterations regarding the vehicle will be on record somewhere, meaning that someone else will be able to gain access to that information. Also, if you are known to have a penchant for certain types of vehicles (say, sports cars) or a specific make, choose something different as the vehicle for the new you. If you happen to be a member of a drivers club, do not make the mistake of maintaining ties with the club once you move to a new area. Do not even rejoin such clubs using your new name!

False Clues

Some people or organizations can be "thrown" if you leave deliberately false indications as to your intended destination or reasons for vanishing. It can sometimes pay to file an official mail-redirection application, giving fictitious details. A letter of explanation left for a spouse, friend, or relative can create a lot of hassles for someone who might use that information to try to find you. The key to success here is to *not* give information which can be readily disproven. For example, do not write that you are going to live with a cousin in London, England. It would be a simple matter for anyone to verify or disprove whether or not you really do have a cousin in that area, expending little time and expense in so doing. A far better bet is to drop a few hints throughout a letter. For example, you can say you're "going to start again with Carol." By the time someone has cross-referenced everything in an attempt to find out who Carol might be and whether you are with her or not, your real trail should be nicely cold. The expense generated by following false leads will eventually deter your tracker from further investigation.

Remember that all companies carry insurance against rip-offs, and unless you owe literally thousands of pounds or dollars, most companies will invest only a tiny percentage in trying to locate you should you disappear without paying your debts. It is more likely that the company to whom you owe the money will sell the debt at a reduction to a debt collection/tracing agency. These firms usually deal with only very large debts, and they can afford to invest *more* money in trying to recover money owed. However, if you have taken all possible precautions against being found, and if you are a good distance from the area in which the debt was incurred, you will *not* be found. A survey of debt-collection agencies in England, Australia, and New Zealand indicated the trend is toward self-employed debt collectors/tracers, meaning that the operative does not get paid unless he actually locates the debtor. This indicates that most companies consider the chances of recovering a debt from someone who has vanished to be extremely slim. The bottom line is that *anything* which might connect the old you with the new one should be changed or abandoned. Imagine what steps you would take if you were trying to find someone, create obstacles to those steps, and you have parried the blow before it is struck.

CONCLUSION

It can be seen from the foregoing chapters that changing one's identity is not as difficult as one might think—despite the efforts of those who seek to prevent such practices. But why would anyone bother? The year 1984 has come and gone, and, for the most part, things seem very much like they always were. And, one suspects, much as they will always be. Technology has changed, of course, but not the motivation or intent of those who consider individual privacy to be at best unnecessary and at worst a genuine threat to the stability and security of "their" country, state, city, or company.

Various dictionaries define *private* and *privacy* as "withdrawn or kept from society, kept or removed from public interest or knowledge, personal and confidential." It takes but a moment's thought to conclude that unless an individual has taken positive steps to not conform with government requirements, or has lived, since his unrecorded birth, in a cave or on a desert island, there has never been any such animal as "privacy." A certain amount of personal privacy must, of course, be sacrificed if one is to take advantage of the various government-sponsored benefits available to citizens of civilized countries. Similarly, some privacy must be given up in order that the police and military may adequately serve and protect the community. This situation has existed for a considerable period of time, so then the question is, what *has* changed?

Well, first of all, recent technological advances have made it possible to almost instantaneously transfer information from place to place—nationally or internationally. The storage and retrieval of that information is now on a massive scale. Records that a decade ago would have taken years to compile can now be established within seconds. The availability and relatively low cost of such equipment has led to its exploitation by persons who, for whatever reason, desire to possess as much personal information about others as is possible. Some of the reasons are valid, but many agencies—public and private—seek such information for its own sake and are prepared to buy, sell, or swap the gathered information. Such firms store the information *in case* it is ever needed—in case you apply for a loan, in case you decide to run for election, or, just in case!

Individuals are increasingly concerned with what they consider an invasion of their privacy when so many details are centrally compiled in a computer system. While I am a firm believer in the need for secrecy (as practiced by the military or intelligence agencies), I do not believe in secrecy for its own sake. If there is nothing to be *lost* by divulging information, I am of the firm belief that it should be freely available to all who desire it. As an example of pointless secrecy, I can use the example of the list of British garages that have had their vehicle-testing status revoked for bad workmanship, malpractice, or for other reasons. This information is classified for some bizarre reason by the British government, and private citizens are not permitted to see the records or request information from them. However, exactly the same information is available from certain American government departments, so that a suitably motivated British citizen can travel to the United States and legally examine copies of the relevant files there!

Although I am an advocate of the principle of freedom of information, it is a fool who believes that any organization or government department will reveal *all* the material it possesses on a given subject, simply because you may have a legal right to it. I have secured certain documents that, up until recently, have been classified under the Official Secrets Act. Although I had no problems obtaining the documents, it is painfully obvious that parts of them have been deleted or reclassified. Of course, such practices are not denied by government departments, but it shows that there is no such thing as "freedom of information" nor, in my opinion, will there ever be.

As computer technology continues to invade personal privacy and liberty, there develops a growing need for information with which individuals can fight back, or a at least parry a few of the blows. This section of the book, therefore, includes many references to computers as they pertain to our private lives. It can be considered a fairly loose assemblage of ideas, thoughts, and techniques, all of which will be of help if and when you decide to change your identity or create a new one.

Despite the seemingly amazing feats performed by computers in society today, they are still only machines, and even the so-called expert programs currently under evaluation will never be able to replicate the performance of a skilled, thinking human under all circumstances. Given the choice between a team of human investigators and the world's most powerful computer, I would choose the humans every time. There is just no contest. If I were the subject at the pointed end of an investigation, I would be really pleased to hear that computers were being employed to collate facts and establish a case against me!

It is important to remember that whereas a human operative might recall a name or address or the color of someone's eyes, a computer will "remember" only what it is programmed to—nothing more. It cannot think, reason, or "feel" that something is wrong, relying solely on the skill of the programmer to provide it with all the information needed to preform its allotted task. In fact, it is the program and not the machine itself that should be considered when evaluating the ability of such systems. At best, programs are rapid, accurate back-ups for human effort. At worst, they are rapid, inaccurate substitutes. In any case, *all* systems have flaws; failings, as it were. Discover these failings, and you have found an open door. Where that door leads is up to you!

Defeating Computer Systems

Imagine, if you will, that you have applied for a loan from your local bank and that the manager has called you to his office for an interview. At this interview, he hopes to establish why you need the money, whether or not you can afford to pay it back, and so on. You are sitting rather nervously in the office, awaiting the manager's arrival. He enters the room, smiles benignly, and the interview begins.

Now, it should come as no surprise when I say that even if your reasons for the loan are justified, your income is good, and your ability to pay excellent, there is no guarantee that you will get the loan. The length of your hair, the color of your skin, your accent—even the way you sit in a chair—will all affect the manager's decision. But a computer functions logically all of the time, having no bad or good days, and executes the current program. If the information put into the computer falls within its operating parameters and the program deems it to be acceptable, it will be accepted—no questions asked.

For example, you can "tell" the American Express computer that you are white, age thirty-four, earn $2000 a week, and have an important job with a local manufacturing company. The computer has no way of checking to see whether you really are as you say you are, and it will therefore accept your statements as true. The only cross-referencing the computer can do is with other computers! If *they* support your claims, you are in. Work volume prevents manual cross-referencing or checking except in very important situations; as the volume of work increases, that which is considered very important becomes less so.

Computers will only ever "know" as much about you as someone else tells them! They are no more sinister than the people who control them, and ultimately that is you. Of course, if you have already given more information than you would have liked to various computer files, your only way out is to start again—with a clean disk. Give only the details that *you* want others to know, and give false information wherever possible. Even seemingly innocent situations can lead to the sale or swapping of your name, address, or other information by one of the computer-file companies. (A small purchase from a shop where the salesman asks for your address so that the company can send you a catalog should, for example, be treated with suspicion.)

It is interesting to note that most larger companies and many government departments that in the course of their daily business send out countless letters, applications, and reminders are aware of the negative reaction generated by computer technology among the average citizens. Consequently, they use "mailmerge"-type programs to create the illusion that the correspondence has been prepared, written, and sent by a human—rather than the series of machines that has actually done so. The better of these systems is very convincing, while the cheaper versions are obvious and tacky. You have probably received examples of both in your junk mail, but there is a definite trend toward their use by licensing departments and other overworked, understaffed government bodies. Watch out for such letters, as they are a sure indication that the department with whom you are dealing has sacrificed most, if not all, of the "personal touch" for increased efficiency!

Very slight differences in print style or quality and grammatical structure can often indicate that the letter has been sent by a machine. A common example of the merge between a standard form letter and your personal details—accomplished by computer program—would be as follows:

Dear Mr. Woodrow:
We notice from our files that a broadcast license for 785 Greenly Street has not yet been issued. As you know, Mr Woodrow, late payment incurs a penalty of...

The computer would have searched for data confirming that the "broadcast license" had been issued. When no such data was found, the program instructed the computer to print the listed name and address onto a standard form. The form would have been fed into a folder, then to an enveloper (the printer would have already addressed the envelope correctly); and it would then be fed to the "out" bin, ready for mailing. Chances are that no human even knows "Mr. Woodrow" exists at this stage. Only if confirmation that the license had been purchased was not input to the computer within an allotted time scale would a "signal" be sent to the human operators. The signal would simply be another printout. Systems such as this are commonplace, and the one described above would be considered *very* basic indeed by state-of-the-art standards.

Apart from the previously mentioned "flaws" in computerized systems, there are two additional factors which make them far less threatening than their card-and-paper counterparts. Firstly, computer security is, and will remain for the foreseeable future, a joke. Oh yes, those that have a vested interest in convincing you of the opposite, and those that have already been convinced—at inestimable cost—will deny the fact, but there it is. There is *no* such thing as a completely secure computer system, and at the bottom end of the scale, computerized records are far easier to access and alter than similar information stored in written or printed form that is kept behind lock and key. Though "hackers" have received some publicity of late, it is the hackers that we do not hear about that concern computer-security chiefs, for these hackers are the ones that know *more* than those that would stop them. Banks, government departments, and private companies regularly lose large amounts of cash or business information to persons who enter their systems, but such entries are not publicized because of the inevitable loss of public confidence. These organizations spend more money having their systems upgraded, the hackers develop more advanced techniques for accessing these systems, and so the cycle continues. As computer technology continues its ingress into everyday life (especially the home), more and more people will develop the skills required to access computer records and remove or alter the information therein. The number of people that can do this— or do it— already runs into thousands. Hackers, by tradition, do so for fun! How many people, past or present, have bothered to physically break into record offices and change or remove information, and of those that have, how many have gotten away with it?

Even I, with my strictly amateur computer skills, have learned enough to be able to enter distant offices, search through records, and alter or remove information stored there without detection—without even leaving home! No doubt as interest in such activity increases, experts in their own field will start to produce books on the subject. Word will spread and, at *that* point, the fun will really start!

Speculation abounds concerning the probable changes in laws and techniques relating to I.D. It is obvious that restrictions and regulations will increasingly make it harder, in theory, to obtain new I.D., but in practice the real problem—work volume at government or other official offices—will not be solved. Although regulations may exist, it will not be possible to put them to effective use. The average citizen will not accept the delays and humiliation necessary for total security. Therefore, those who implement recommended procedures will be forced to compromise. In any case, the trend is toward the computerization of records and information. As I have already mentioned, in terms of security, such a trend is regressive.

I know that terrorist and extremist groups use "new I.D." to move unhindered around their target areas, and that worries me. I have been on the receiving end of terrorist attacks, and it makes one paranoid to wonder about the identity of that stranger in the car outside your window. What is worse is the knowledge that, when asked, the "stranger in the car" will be able to produce a range of genuine and valid identification documents, none of which will come up dirty on a "suspect" or "known" list.

Short of tatooing everyone's forehead with an I.D. code, or forcing everyone to have a small I.D. transmitter injected into his skin, there really is no way of ensuring that people are who they claim to be. Even if I.D. cards are replaced with computer-printed titanium disks bearing holograms of the holder's fingerprints, what supportive documents would be required in order that citizens may apply for such disks? It is too late to introduce new techniques to counter errant individuals; any methods of I.D. issue and reference implemented now will be aimed at preventing abuse by future generations. In the context of curtailing terrorism and other criminal activities, the effect will be minimal. In regard to personal

GENERAL TECHNIQUES AND INFORMATION

freedom and liberty—good old-fashioned privacy—the effects will be frightening. Or will they? Future generations will know only the system they grow up with and, by that time, punishing the many to get at the few may be par for the course. Many commentators will, of course, point out that books such as this help—even encourage—criminals by providing them with valuable information with which they may defeat the system. My belief is that such books do *more* to prevent abuses, close loopholes, or expose failings than do a hundred reports compiled by nine-to-five bureaucrats.

I.D. Quick Reference Chart

The list below shows which commonly used I.D. can be obtained in the countries covered within this book and what evidential identification can be shown in order to secure it. In all countries, excluding England, it is recommended you first obtain a birth certificate.

ENGLAND

DRIVER'S LICENSE	No evidential I.D. is required.
N.I. NUMBER	No evidential I.D. is required. Some supportive I.D. will help.
BIRTH CERTIFICATE	No evidential I.D. is required.
MEDICAL CARD	No evidential I.D. is required. Some supportive I.D. will help.
VISITOR'S PASSPORT	Birth certificate or similar (see application) plus photos.
NATIONAL'S PASSPORT	Birth certificate, referee's statement, plus photos.
UNION CARD	No I.D. is required for most unions.

AUSTRALIA

BIRTH CERTIFICATE	No evidential I.D. is required. Supportive I.D. will help.
SOCIAL SECURITY NUMBER	Evidential I.D. is required for all applications to DSS.
DRIVER'S LICENSE	Proof of age may be required.
PASSPORT	Birth certificate, referee's statement, photos.
STUDENTS I.D. CARD	Where I.D. is required, tutor's declaration and employer's reference are often used.

NEW ZEALAND

BIRTH CERTIFICATE	No evidential I.D. is required. Application form.
DRIVER'S LICENSE	New Zealand citizens need a birth certificate; nonnationals, birth certificate or passport.
SOCIAL SECURITY NUMBER	Evidential I.D. is required of persons dealing with Social Welfare Department.
PASSPORT	Birth certificate, photos, identification certificate (see application).
MEDICAL CARD	Evidential I.D. is not required for most private insurance schemes.

CANADA

BIRTH CERTIFICATE	Evidential I.D. may be requested by individual officers at registry.
SOCIAL INSURANCE NUMBER	Birth certificate and one other piece of I.D. (license, rent receipts, etc.)
MEDICAL CARD	Private medical insurance companies rarely require evidential I.D.
DRIVER'S LICENSE	Birth certificate and one other piece of I.D.
PASSPORT	Birth certificate, photos, guarantor's statement or Form PPT 132.